Collected Poems

PETER MCDONALD was born in Belfast in 1962, and was educated at Methodist College, Belfast, and University College, Oxford. After winning the Newdigate Prize and an Eric Gregory Award, he published his first book of poems in 1989. His critical and editorial work includes *Mistaken Identities: Poetry and Northern Ireland* (1997), *Serious Poetry: Form and Authority from Yeats to Hill* (2002), *The Collected Poems of Louis MacNeice* (2007), and *Sound Intentions: The Workings of Rhyme in Nineteenth-Century Poetry* (2012). He is the editor of W.B. Yeats' *Complete Poems* for Longman. For the last thirty years Peter McDonald has divided his time between Northern Ireland and England, where he works as a university lecturer at Christ Church, Oxford. He has two children, and lives in Oxfordshire.

Also by Peter McDonald from Carcanet Press

Pastorals
The House of Clay
Torchlight

PETER McDONALD

Collected Poems

CARCANET

First published in Great Britain in 2012 by

Carcanet Press Limited
Alliance House
Cross Street
Manchester M2 7AQ

www.carcanet.co.uk

Biting the Wax was first published by Bloodaxe Books, Northumberland, 1989
Adam's Dream was first published by Bloodaxe Books, Northumberland, 1996

A CIP catalogue record for this book is available from the British Library

ISBN 978 1 84777 098 1

The publisher acknowledges financial assistance from Arts Council England

Typeset by XL Publishing Services, Tiverton
Printed and bound in England by SRP Ltd, Exeter

For my children

Louisa and Samuel

Contents

Biting the Wax (1989)

The Dog 3
Paprika 4
Ether 4
Short Story 5
Some Figures 6
Cash Positive 7
Still 7
Wrong 8
Galatea 8
The Twilight Summit 9
Count Dracula Entertains 10
Deception 10
A Gift 11
Swimmer 12
First Light 13
Out of Ireland 14
Ideal Home 15
The Signal 15
The South 16
Killers 17
In the Hall of Mirrors 17
Silent Night 18
Grace Before Meat 22
Survivors 22
China 23
A Volume of Memoirs is Forthcoming 24
Mahogany 25
Still Life 25
A Prism 26
Tercets 26
The Deaf Wars 27
Totalled 28
The Hands of Juan Peron 29
The Green, Grassy Slopes of the Boyne 31
The Third Day 33
Sunday in Great Tew 34

Adam's Dream (1996)

The Situation 41
Meissen 41
On a Good Day 42
Reno 43
Endtime 44
Breakfast 45
Bitter 45
The Brancusi Room 46
A Hard Place 47
The Glen 47
The Creatures 48
Peacetime 49
Five Circumstances 50
From the Porch 51
An Eclipse 52
The Passions 53
Delaval 54
On Show 55
The Glass Harmonica 56
About Lisbon 56
The Earthquake 57
Academic Sentences
  1 First Principles 57
  2 Point A 58
  3 Eidolon 59
  4 Walking in the Garden 61
  5 Point B 62
Adam's Dream 63
De Gustibus 66
The Authorities 66
A Pause 67
The Rival 67
The Dedication 68
In the Sketchbook 68
The Aftermath 69
In His Place 69
Lines on the Demolition of the *Adelphi*, 1937 70

Pastorals (2004)

Two Trees 73
The Cup 74
A Gloss 75
Visitors 75
At Castlereagh Church 76
Pastoral 76
The Scald 77
Air and Angels 78
Work: 1958 79
Foreknowledge 80
The Victory Weekend
Friday 80
Saturday 82
Sunday 86
Least Harm 89
A History Channel 89
The Resurrection of the Soldiers 90
Two Memorials at Gilnahirk 91
Spillage 92
Words for a Poem 92
The Cloud 93
August 93
At Rosses Point 94
Travellers 94
The Long Look 95
The Road to Rome 95
An Alarm 101
The Blood-Bruise 101
Standstill 102
A Fall 102
The Conversion 103
The Risk 103
The Mild Autumn 104
Two Spiders 105
Hush 105
Seashells 106
The Full House 106
Work: 1998 107
The Stand-Off 108

The Thread 108
Damon the Mower 109
The Way to Lose 109
Fireworks 110
Eclogue 112
The Company 115
The Proof 116
The Back Roads 116
The Watercolourists 117

THE HOUSE OF CLAY (2007)

San Domenico 121
The Hand 122
As Seen 124
Cetacea 126
Clearout 127
The Gnat 128
Literal 129
War Diary 130
The Moth 131
The Other World 132
Strongman 132
Spoils 133
The Overcoat 134
A Schoolboy 136
Windows 137
Three Rivers
Isis 138
Lagan 139
Jordan 139
The Pattern 140
Syrian 142
The Fob-Watch 143
Against the Fear of Death 144
Mar Sarkis 145
In Heaven 146
The Anniversary 147
Inventory 148
Forecast 149

Flex 149
The Walk 150
Quis Separabit 151
Late Morning 152
The Pieces 153
The Street Called Straight 158
Arithmetic 158
Vigilantes 159
Ode 160
44A 160
The Bees 163
Coda 166

TORCHLIGHT (2011)

The Neighbours 169
The Weather 169
Singles 170
Reversing Around a Corner 171
Rainbow Ribbons 1980 172
The Reeds 172
Green Tea 173
A Pair of Shoes 175
Oxford Poetry 176
The Interruption 178
Draught 179
Canopic Jars
- 1 Lights 180
- 2 Liver 180
- 3 Intestines 181
- 4 [Heart] 181

Slowest 182
Portrush 183
Later 183
Augury 184
A Castaway 185
The Difference 186
The Harbour 187
Penalty 188
Hymn 188

The Wait 203
Sappho fr. 58 203
Country 204
Riddarsholmskyrkan 211
Broken 211
Least 212
Childhood Memories
  1 The Battery Boy 213
  2 1966 213
  3 Souvenir d'Ypres 214
  4 Torchlight 214
  5 Blue Skies 215
  6 Petrol 215
  7 Bits and Pieces 216
  8 The Collar 216
  9 Kenneth 217
  10 Spartans 217
  11 Saturday 218
  12 Tommy 218
This Earth 219
The Cheetah 220

Notes 225
Index of Titles 233
Index of First Lines 239

BITING THE WAX

1989

The Dog

The dog lay there with one leg missing,
dead apparently, right in front of the door
all morning. We came out to move it,
but a crowd from somewhere catcalled and hissed,
then a stone or two clattered past us, hit
the window, took a chunk out of the wall.
We retreated, and the dog still lay there.
Silence from outside echoed in the hall.

That night, it was dogs barking everywhere,
glass crunching on the road. The TV
spat and flickered for an hour or more
until the pictures stopped, as suddenly
as lights blacked out and the phone died.
We must have fumbled with matches and candles,
for we made out windows shaking, handles
tried on the strong doors. Then voices outside.

The troublemakers wouldn't show their faces
until the very last, so it was said.
The only time they'll look you in the eye
(patterns of plaster on the sheepskin rug)
it's then you'll know that you're as good as dead.
Still carpeted, the flat felt like a safe place
most days, although at night the noises started
and the locks got stronger. Now there was the dog.

At last, peace: dawn and a spreading silence,
fires burning out, maybe a car passing
and little else to be heard. By midday
one of us had emerged, and was standing
on a littered path, swiping the flies away.
The dog was there still, and the smell of the dog.
He called back, *An accident*. In the distance,
a helicopter with one blade missing.

Paprika

Behind them, the radio surges
its way into the conversation.
Early evening, and the noise of Europe
is Babel's atmospherics,

the sound of dust and headaches.
Rising in the half-dark
they close a window, make coffee,
try to hold down the signal.

Florence this summer. And next
year somewhere new – down
the Rhine, Hungary maybe,
or that tour of Yugoslavia.

The birds are deafening, the radio
white noise by now, and even
the coffee is burning their tongues.
Something terrible is going to happen.

Ether

Those lovers in the attic
who scratch and cry their way
out of each other's lives
gradually the night through
until at dawn they sleep,
are becoming the soundtrack
for the worst of our bad dreams,
those separate B-movies
where the lumbering, hurt monsters
turn out to be ourselves.

I look inside your lovers' heads
to where you lie naked,

frozen blue on the soil,
and lurch away in terror
through mist and huge trees,
still hearing the first of your cries,
your moans, and gasps, and silences.
A brute, my hands fumble
from trunk to trunk, as if
the damp wood kept you there.

Kneeling at a rain pool
and about to catch the water,
I can tap your snow-dream
through fathoms of ether:
silence, but for the crack
and groan of ice
further and further north;
some creature's wounded howl
for a face that shatters
at the drop of one hand.

Short Story

At last there was time to dream again,
or it seemed that way at least:
the sunset had changed only slightly
since yesterday, but it had changed.

The photograph he tried for became
a letter, and the letter became ash
in his own hearth before long,
even before the sun had set.

There was always something else to be caught,
or there would be soon, with luck;
his fire burned like the sun in Florida

where, slightly drunk by now, the last
astronaut alive was still wondering
how to make his way back to the moon.

Some Figures

The clouds were following one another south
and we were following the clouds, as if
that were the reasonable thing to do,
slowly for days, then slowly for a month,
feeling the ice begin to lace our breath
like men who had already come to grief
and were buried now in air and sea-snow.

But pressing on required no special skill:
the nights were full of drink, the days morose
and broody, staring down to a thick sea,
awaiting the time of arbitrary landfall,
then wading ashore in ones and twos, until
we stood, wrapped up like spacemen, close
together, in ourselves a single colony.

I think perhaps we wanted to begin again,
to have another try at that new start,
but the ice and sleet, as we huddled there together,
were making for cohesion, and the pain
involved in staying close seemed less in vain
than that of separation, being torn apart
to strike out freely, far from one another.

And so we stayed, and froze into our places
as snow-sculptures, first with faces half-defined,
then bolder, heavier forms with curious features,
and finally as abstract things, where traces
of figure or line are conjectural, and surfaces
are white and changing, leaving nothing behind
to hold us all accountable as living creatures.

Cash Positive

Two telephones all morning giving each other hell
in the highest office between here and God,
a desk polished black so you can see your face
and a silent screen that flashes messages

across cities, oceans and thousands of miles;
a printer beside it zipping away, murmuring
at intervals all day in different inks:
nobody says much except to the telephones.

I'd start by talking about securities,
though nobody is ever safe, and things
get sticky, dangerous – you might even
pick up something nasty from the keyboard

or the one love of your life, just think of that –
and what reply *is* there anyway
to the fax's cruel jibing, its clever *This*
is the promised land calling, the poor boy on the line?

Still

Clutching his sides at the very mention of the name,
he looks, caught there, as though he might be
preparing either to laugh or to cry his heart out.

Around him most of the others are stony faced,
fixing their gazes on a point some seven feet
from the floor on the one wall that isn't there.

Only the dark-haired girl is beginning to respond,
raising spread palms, opening her eyes wide
and training them just clear of his left shoulder.

Although there's no sign of the unexpected guest
inside the frame, he'll still be around somewhere,
keeping close to the wall, probably, just about here.

Wrong

Even if she had asked him, the blue girl, what
she might say or do just at that moment
or how she could ever ask the right way of things,
even if the music had stopped, or at least
had become softer, then there might have been a chance;
as it was, the spotlights flashed over her cheeks,
over her shoulders and back, the blue of her hair,
the music dropped down on top of her like lead
and down from the ceiling a thousand lethal
bubbles came floating, then confetti and streamers
came down and burned her; everything, even
the lights and the cold were pointing to the same
conclusion, and then of course her colours changed:
even the doorman was seen to wipe a tear
away with the finger of one white glove
as if, with that gesture, he too might bring the house down.

Galatea

Each night when they bring her face to face
with her torturers, when she
and the branding iron come cheek to cheek,
he's in his box, watching from behind a curtain,
and before retrieving his coat and top hat
from the headless lackey, will have closed
his eyes just as she and the hot iron
kiss, opening them in time for her screams
and the rest of the action, live on stage.

Is he quite sure she felt no pain?
Alone at night in his private chamber
of horrors, locked in with her waxwork double,
he gives his doctor's hands
the run of her body, smoothing out
blemishes and talking as a lover might do,

allowing himself one classical allusion
as he starts to unbutton Galatea's dress,
biting the wax, abject, *surréaliste*.

The Twilight Summit

Imagine the scene:
it's one of those places in Donegal
where the Volvos never bother to stop,
and this pub's more of a dance-hall
that's empty, near enough, all afternoon:
a cave for drinking in,
a cave of making and dreaming,
more real than O'Hagan's paper-shop
or the road from here to Bundoran.

A pair of hardened *raconteurs*
are busy finding the words
to measure the distance between them:
each leans and leers towards
a bar where the different ambers
of two pints dwindle, beside them
each a glowing talisman
of Bush or Jameson,
where nation speaks unto nation.

By now, those hoarse, raised voices
are echoing so much
around this blacked-out dance-floor
that neither of them really hears
what it is the other's saying:
there's one last lunge and clutch
at a glass, and here comes more,
though nobody knows who's paying.
Good man yourself, then. Cheers!

Count Dracula Entertains

Unfortunately, it was never simple,
though for years now you've been dreaming
of wonderful solutions. Did I scare you?
I have this habit of coming through
just at the wrong time, like other things,
hunger, love, sleep for example.

Forgive the accent: you will understand
what it's like to be a foreigner abroad
or, for that matter, an alien at home,
where you curse it all, to the last bomb
waiting its moment on some empty road
that stretches out into the back of beyond

– which is my country too, of course,
completely surrounded by one blank sea
we call oblivion, despair.
Maybe one day you could spend some time there:
it's just the place to write your poetry,
to go to the bad, and then to worse.

Our comforts, I'm afraid, will be few
and simple, but you'll still have your visions
– a tree of light, then nothing but light –
and I'll still have my victims every night,
for ours would be the finest of collusions:
the best dreams are of dreams coming true.

Deception

The narrow channel they call Neptune's Bellows
leads into Whaler's Bay, a lava beach
where tin cans from the fifties and big bones
are leftovers with few now to disturb them
along the dull fringes of Deception Island.

Mostly the penguins come and go, often
a conclave of fur seals makes an appearance,
and sometimes you can pick out human figures
among the oil tanks and dead furnaces,
like wanderers with nowhere left to go
who wind up here, the last place on God's earth.
They'll be scientists, perhaps, or crazy tourists
on a trip from Cape Horn to the South Shetlands,
viewing the litter and the whaling relics
in summer weather. They leave their marks, too:
soft-drink and vodka bottles, petrol cans,
or bold graffiti written out in Spanish,
signatures scattered among the other last things
where a rock by the sea reads *Death To Pinochet.*

A Gift

The maker of necklaces turns his back
on the latest customer. Before
you go, take this: silver and black,
a string of glass from London,
hand-worked silver, pebbles black to the core.

In the car doing ninety,
England is peaceful, the past
no more than a minute's sky,
neutral, nothing to do with us.
We stop to the smell of petrol
and hot rubber, home at last.

With my one hand holding a glass,
the other ponders the intricate
weight of your necklace.
For a moment, I hesitate
before I speak, at one almost
with the heat of four black tyres,
the sky, the smell of petrol,
with the customer, and the maker of necklaces.

Swimmer

Stung, twisting in
and out of himself, he
gapes into the current,

swallowing its weight
to drag himself down
towards that continent,

an unmapped green
tortured with voices,
opening up, closing

over him. He can hear
his own voice bubble:
everything is possible

and probable;
for the dreamer, there are
no secrets, no illusions,

no laws. His fish-
eye could let her swim
back into the world,

holding the tiny
pebbles of Valium
safe in her palm.

The writing on her letters
runs, a hard smear
over the roof of light

that splinters, as
he dives upwards,
gasping in the air

of wherever she waits
for a stranger
to come from the water,

into summer heat
and a dull
mirage-shimmer

over the riverbank.
He climbs to a place
where everything is possible

as the sky levels
all its long spaces
to a dream of water.

First Light

Already, on the hills,
men are at work, tending
animals and whistling softly
to themselves. In a field
nearby, two horses
crop the grass lazily.

Elsewhere, coming out
of hiding, the professional
hunters have won again.
They rest in a clearing
and light cigarettes
as blood steams in the sun –

a neutral light
and silence that could yet
fill with music;
the alien sweetness
of nightingales (there has
been talk of violence,

madness); or the swan's
last aria coming through
from springs high up
where fresh water
will break from rock
when the death-song is over.

About a mile off coast
a single yacht is leaning
into the spray.
Its sails fill
with the whole weight of morning
as it turns away.

Euripides, *Phaethon*

Out of Ireland

Just how far do you have to go
before you get to the world's edge?
Today, a hard sun lights the snow
for miles, and deep inside his cage

your tame canary sings and dances,
ignoring winter. He has a voice
and uses it, taking no chances:
he entertains, as though he had a choice.

This summer you'll be sailing west,
whether the sea is calm or angry,
until you drop. Your bird knows the rest,
he knows he'll die hungry.

Ideal Home

As soon as you open the front door
on to a deep-pile hall carpet
and harvest-gold walls,
you begin the new life.
In the lounge, you sit
smoking, as your wife
fixes some drinks, maybe cocktails.
Already you're asking for more.

It's been like this from the start:
a kitchen that almost runs itself,
the TV, the sleeping video.
In case of emergencies
the basement has enough
food for twenty days,
a purring clock-radio
and an ashtray the shape of a heart.

The Signal

It seemed too long to wait, and the queue, a dozen deep,
barely moved in half an hour, so he took his hat and left,
went to open the glass door to the traffic and the people
in their winter coats and hats, when the man behind him laughed

and he looked and there behind him was another beard and coat
and another and another, and the heavy glass sighed shut,
for the people would not look, and he knew that he'd been caught
when the men came into focus with their faces grey like slate.

But the queue itself was silent, and he wondered whether now
it was time for him to speak, to ring a bell or cry for help,
though he kept his mouth shut all the same, because he knew
that the orders and sub-clauses in his case gave no hope.

No hope for him of moving any further now than back
to the queue of coats and beards, this time to the very end,
and his own face was like slate, and the slate about to break,
and the pieces when they broke would fall away and not be found.

So he stood his ground like Simeon, his beard began to grow
as the rain blattered and blurred the glass world of the door
where no one spoke or moved, and the light stopped coming
through
when his silence rose in silence, broke in darkness like a flare.

The South

The story may not be true, of course: that pair
who'd lived too close to an airbase, or seen one
too many documentaries where bombs
exploded a mile over the dome of St Paul's;
panicked, they hauled an atlas from the shelf
and searched out data on prevailing winds,
on rainfall, tides, and all the likely targets.
They came up with a location far to the south
as the safest place in either hemisphere,
sold up and moved there, having chosen then
(a year before that episode was played)
the Falkland Islands in the South Atlantic.

Each time you hear that easy parable
it changes, gains or loses from the teller,
his sense of detail, or her sense of timing
(of course, a lot depends upon the punchline).
The best response to a story is to cap it
with a better of your own; let's say the year
you found yourself on ice, much further south,
in the shifting deserts of Antarctica:
the Chilean aeroplane refuses to land,
so here you stay, stuck at a weather station,
listening for the news from the Malvinas,
a thousand miles from here to anywhere.

Killers

You could think of them as hunters,
achieved, professional,
ready for anything.
Their minds are on the job in hand
and their hands are steady.
They've gone by now, most likely,

but in the country, one by one,
the birds are falling
out of the sky, into
another shade of green;
just sparrows, thrushes,
nothing exceptional,

at least nothing you'd notice
in this weather, walking
the wet road home
at closing time, until
there are hands on your arm,
light as feathers.

In the Hall of Mirrors

To think that it should come to this,
seeing my own eyes stare me in the face
where the bigger I get the smaller I become,
vice versa, in a flash. Nobody said
anything about this, or what it's worth
to you, or me, or anyone.
And how many mirrors would they need,
how few could they get away with?

The strip-lights flicker up like nerves
on all the miles of motorway
through the skulls of these giants and dwarfs,

assorted spooks and goons; but why
should my feet be rhyming with my head
on glass, like razor-blades with spoons?

Silent Night

Jersey, 1946

It's summer now, or nearly. Out at the back door, my sister
shows the children how to feed birds, scattering pieces
of crust into the garden: some sparrows, a couple of starlings
come down and squabble, fly off at the children's applause.
In the bathroom, I'm weighing myself – another stone – smiling,
hearing my name called, catching the smells from the kitchen.

Those weeks when they came to take my story for the wireless
I had to be coaxed at first; they seemed to be after
more than names, or names and facts; they wanted to know
how it felt then, and sounded, what it tasted and smelled like,
though really it was like nothing, nothing before or since,
which I told them, and they said they understood. But even so.

But even so, as they added, there was a story to be told,
and I was the man to tell it. First, there were questions
and answers, *What did you see then? And what were you thinking?*
But after a while, the story would come of its own accord
and there were the details they wanted, the smells and the sounds,
memories that never made sense, for once locking into each other.

The first place they took you. At Wilhelmshaven that winter,
when every afternoon repeated the frost of the morning,
and at night there was only hail to cut into the tracks
of their lights, they bundled me with a couple of dozen
newcomers into one of the big 'huts', my feet touching
the ground for the first time since the court-martial in Jersey.

How many in this hut? There were nearly a thousand,
crammed three to a bed, head to toe in the bunks and making
barely a sound. Near enough a thousand men. Packed
that tightly, you soon learn to sleep without moving,
and you learn not to speak, to lie still and say nothing
when guards are on hand to force up the value of silence.

It was part of Neuengamme, and I had been brought over
from France with the others – Jean De Frotté, Bernard
Depuy, just to give two names as examples: the first one
tall, wispy-haired and delicate, the son of a Marquis,
then Bernard with his square head screwed down to his shoulders:
they have their stories, still different, still parts of mine.

We had three things to talk about: food, sleep and work,
but no real need to think, for these were all taken care of,
especially the last. Once a day, thin turnip soup
and a crust of bread, a few hours of motionless sleep,
then a hard tramp through frost out to the Kriegsmarine
Arsenal, a day's work to the punch and clang of the riveters,

avoiding welders' blue clouds of sparks; sweat and iron;
then our convicts' shuffle back to the camp in the dark,
their searchlights tailing us and filling in the distance
back to the gates, our hut with its three hundred bunks.
I mentioned guards: there were guards of course, but worse
were the chiefs, one to each hut. Ours was called Omar.

It turned out that he had once, like most of the others,
been a prisoner himself, a young man when they caught him
in 1933, some would-be radical journalist.
He had been through worse in his day, worse beatings,
work, cold, and the rest, and he was in for a lifetime.
Drop by drop, I expect, the fight just bled out of him.

So once the camps were getting busy they made him an offer,
to serve his time as an *Alteste* in places like Neuengamme
with at least enough freedom there to do as he pleased
and get on with the job. Yes, the words apply, yes brutal,
just like the others, sadistic. And yes, there are stories.
I try to remember my friend Bernard's straight talking,

'There's no point in judging a place like this by the standards
of what we've all left behind: it has a code of its own,
a lunatic code, I know, but you just have to learn it.
Lie still and say nothing.' So what is there for me to say now
about Omar? Just the truth, just what I remember?
But I couldn't call it the truth then, and now that I tell you

the stories, does that make them all true? Does it make them
happen, happen really for the first time? It's harder,
watching the sea relax under the first mild summer evening,
and waiting for dinner, too, harder to force those things
to happen again, and here, than just to keep silent, or lie.
Here by the bay, in fact there's no such thing as silence,

what with the waves breaking all night, and the seabirds
carrying on as usual each day. On the wireless, they tell me,
you can do wonders, but the one thing you can't get away with
is silence, the fretful noise of empty spaces, the worrying
gaps bare of music or talk, with just the sound of the atmosphere
sifting its way to your room. I can give you two stories

concerning Omar, though whether or not they go well together
I myself couldn't say. The first happened only a few weeks
after we arrived at the camp: an Alsatian boy of sixteen
had been caught making off with food scraps from the plates
of patients in the Infirmary (though that was no hospital
as you'd understand the word – a dirty and crowded tin hut).

He came up before Omar, who glared, and let his face buckle
in on itself with disgust, producing the worst of his voices
– the fabulous, wicked giant, incredible even to himself –
then thundered down, 'You, boy, you have committed
the one unforgiveable crime: you've gone and stolen
not just from your comrades, but from your sick comrades.

I'll tell you exactly how you can expect to be punished:
you're going to learn now all the meaning of hunger,
but you'll dread the food in your mouth; when you leave here
you'll be as good as mad, gibbering away in the corner.'
He was perfect: large as life and more monstrous than any
caricature. The boy just cringed and was carried away.

The customary stamping and shouting. Then wet blankets
for him to sleep in, nights on end: they starved him, next
force-fed him salted food, served up on a scalding
hot spoon, day after day, always refusing him water.
By the time they lost interest, he looked like a skeleton;
unable to eat for the burns on his mouth, on his lips and tongue,

he would scream at the sight of a spoon. He didn't last long,
at the end gibbering, as promised. Now I can barely imagine
such things happening at all, but they did, they do still
I suppose, in places far removed from this island,
real horrors, more common knowledge now than before
and more than just hearsay: newsreels, words on the air.

Of course, there's a second *vignette*: the very same Omar
– who was, he would tell you, cultured; had been a classical
musician in his time; still a diehard lover of Mozart –
in 1944, at Christmas, he laid on something special.
Picture a great hut that has been cleared for the purpose,
with benches there now and a stage, the audience silent

(though you wouldn't mistake that for hushed expectation,
since it's clearly enough the schooled silence of fear),
and then you make out a tree just to the right of the stage,
a piano likewise, the feeling of something about to begin.
Suddenly Omar, and six of the other *Altesten*
troop out like schoolboys, with their heavy, straight faces,

and this is a carol service, these fat men are the carollers:
if you listen, you can pick up Omar's gentle booming
among all the voices. It happens that I was arrested
for 'communal listening'; it might be played for the wireless,
but no actor could reproduce the sound of this memory,
such music in the hungry air, *Stille Nacht, heilige Nacht.*

On clear evenings, those rocks on the near side of the bay
are a circle of broken teeth, soon blotted out by the tide.
I listen to birds roosting for miles along the coast,
then there's just the sea noise, and the evening programmes,
the news, good and bad, the music of Victor Sylvester,
the Epilogue, the King; whisper and fizz from the atmosphere.

People are calling me in now: I'll laugh with the children
over this story or that, sometimes catch myself thinking
not of the past exactly, but more of the broadcast,
my voice with the voices of actors, somewhere among them
Jean and Bernard still alive; that carol; the last
winter of a bad war; a boy with a horror of spoons.

Grace Before Meat

A spoon palms, cups her face,
her whole body
displaced on the surfaces
of cutlery. The table
is a written page

where now the knives
might be glancing back at me,
seeming to smile
in the light that carves its way
from edge to clean edge.

Survivors

Next morning, we slip back out
to the garden to gather up.
Sluggish ghosts of cigarettes
are still losing their grip
on the rooms they used, where now
like inoffensive flags,
failures, our curtains flap.

We've cleared inside, somehow,
hangovers notwithstanding,
seen the glasses gathered in
and swept disaster zones
where they tried out their crash-landings,

we've corralled the dead and dying
bottles, and poured away the dregs.

Lastly, the garden here:
damp grass and tramped-in fags,
half-empty beer cans, top-
heavy trees, the sun going in.
Ten minutes more of ending
it all, and the last one standing's
a pushover, a spilt glassful of rain.

China

Just as he'd told them every Christmas,
her father would be dead within the year.
She would marry again within another
and move to a different neck of the woods.
The brother and his wife would have their second daughter.

Distances grew vaster every year:
his death had brought the father no closer,
and her brother came no nearer a son,
so at last the name, too, would go.
Now there was no more really to be done

than to meet up each year at Christmas,
or maybe just every other Christmas,
when they would talk, and she might mention
something of what it was she was after
when the job let her get away,

and even, if the words didn't fail her,
how she had gone the length of China
and walked on the wall
fully a mile
quite recently, just the summer before last.

A Volume of Memoirs is Forthcoming

And now they tell me that the old girl's dying,
stuck on the West coast with that bad third son
who's helping her rewrite the will again;
apparently she's hired some young gun
to ghost the memoirs she's been threatening
for longer now than even I remember.
At nights, she sits up with a tape-recorder
and spits out memories like bitter seeds,
pointing the finger, naming all the names,
telling it like it is, or was, or needs
to be in the long run. Each sick morning
when she's back on her deathbed, and the beads
are clicking away in the bedroom, he sits down
and listens through the night's fresh revelations;
then it's back to tapping words across a screen,
watching the evidence accumulate
in hard green letters, irrefutable.

It can't be long now till the thing's in print,
and I'll be combing the index for my name,
morose and sullen, tight-lipped, miserable,
watching as she helps me to the blame
for everything, for almost everything.
Sometimes I'll wake, much as I do these nights,
and catch in the dark above me a quick glint
from her one green eye, and maybe hear her sing
snatches of ballads that I'd never learn
at her knee, or at the hearthstone; then I'll turn
my face to the wall and shout her ghost down:
already, you see, I've got her in my sights;
I have the material ready now and waiting,
and I start writing tomorrow at dawn.

Mahogany

They drink cold wines by the side of a river
as respite from their table talk, while under
planted trees the quiet flunkeys gather,
comparing notes, half-trusting one another.
It is nearly safe for us to leave them there.

They rise refreshed and hopeful almost
as the entourage slips back indoors, where papers
will have been laid out on the mahogany table,
stacked on their own reflections. Politely,
they sit down again to look at the terrible pictures.

Still Life

Today there's a blind slop of oils
that stops before it's finished

where the ghost of a line trails
through an apple and an empty dish

to pull up exactly seven
inches from your eyes.

(Subversive, it says,
guerrilla even.)

Where the woman sat
with streetlights to see by

once the sun sets,
you can open your eyes now:

a crumpled pink tissue, seven
shades of black and blue.

A Prism

How long is it now since the two of us
stood watching the Irish Sea darken
with hardly a word between us?
I can barely recognise myself; your own
face is long gone,
leaving the sea unchanged behind it.

Things go on changing, all the same:
this morning, for instance,
the season loosens, and I walk away
from my seven colours, into
the forgetful light of spring,
as though, somehow, the new life

were really beginning here
and at last I had forgotten
the darkness waiting like a screen
behind and around me
where still, impossibly,
Richard of York gives battle in vain.

Tercets

Don't wake them; they have been asleep too long,
hooping each other with their open arms
and maybe dreaming. Anyway, leave them.

★

In the same room, saying next to nothing,
you start to hear every sound as it comes
back on itself, and imagine it changes.

★

If they dream of soldiers, are their dreams
cacophonous still with guns and shells, fire
ploughing up fields to sow them with the dead?

*

I can't see well in the dark, but it all
comes back in the end, and you whisper again
Don't wake them now, they've been asleep too long.

The Deaf Wars

It's nearly over now.
I suppose you've broken cover,
though it makes no odds; the words
shrunk back unspoken, long ago,
whatever you meant to say.
There's still maybe a year or two

to go before you tell
the whole truth, such as it is.
Tonight a soldier gets loaded
on a tranquilliser cocktail,
gaping at clouds of roses,
the silent blossoms of shells.

Charlie Chaplin went to France
To teach the cannibals how to dance
and here they come
skipping over the trenches,
each one swinging a time-bomb.
And their theme today is silence.

So the mud has you washed up
on a final high place,
open-mouthed, amazed
in a stalled sign-language
for the last of the comic deaths.
Your smile trickles over the edge.

Totalled

The costumes are a kind of late-colonial,
all primary colours and designer labels;
the hair's worn long and blow-dried, accents
are half-way between here and America;
a badge on his lapel says the producer
WON'T TAKE NO FOR AN ANSWER, and maybe
it's true he has a way with the impossible:
resprayed old cars, given a last polish,
catapult into walls and shop windows,
into each other, they're always totalled,
and right on cue the flames come bursting
just to make everything final;
the sound's dubbed later, of fists connecting,
gunshots, brakes, happy or sad music.

Two men are waiting in a skyline office,
each one silently adding up the other
and playing the razor-cool executive.
The first smoothes a map, points to one corner,
and thinks out all the disadvantages –
it's too late, and impossible anyway
to make much of that sector. He's starting
to speak now, with a shrug in his voice
and his eyes fixed on the middle distance,
part of him slipping out to some margin
where a young achiever jokes in a monotone
of how already he's allowed for losses
and nowadays, in any case, that country
is washed-up, written-off, a place for dead people.

The Hands of Juan Peron

It was going to take four of us at least:
one to kill the floodlights and blind
the cameras whirring at their posts,
another to slip out from behind
the thick-set line of trees and past
the guards' hut, moving from lock to lock
with the quick fingers of a surgeon;
then, and this is where I came in,
for dragging the lead far enough back
from the roof of his bunker coffin,
the services of two or three strong men.

They had set the date for early June,
mentioning things like a rising curve,
a jump in the temperature, tides
having to be taken on the turn;
knowing they would have reasons of their own
as well as reputations to preserve,
all I could do was set a modest price
and say that a poor man sees both sides
no matter what the question;
I told them I never ignored advice,
and yes, I'd always forget a face.

The night when it came was thick with heat,
settled alike over moonlit slums
and the new road, lighted and straight,
that led to the gates and the big trees
swaying at the edge of his estate.
Even here, there was the city noise
and insects, and faint clicks and hums
that came from the gateman's intercom;
beneath us, twigs and gravel gave
the tiniest hints of our presence:
just after midnight, we made our move.

Everything was happening at long distance;
there were maybe fifty or sixty yards
between me and that mausoleum
(a wedding cake in black marble,
swollen up solid with importance),
as I watched the first of two guards
go down, and one man sidle
up to the locked door of the tomb:
he knelt there like a pilgrim
for a matter of seconds, then gave the sign
to bring us out into the open.

Just like in dreams where you run for miles
uphill, towards or away from something,
we were up and into the dead hall
with its musty drapes and flags, its tiles
running cold beneath us all along
the polished path to his resting place.
We climbed the casket like a wall:
a tiny spotlamp had been left on
for a nightlight, and as we looked down
we saw him lying where it shone,
a child in bed, with a waxy face.

From behind us there were shouted whispers,
then a toolbag slung up and caught;
I was pulling him out by the epaulettes,
until his stuffed body with its taut
dried skin, its coiffure and powdered whiskers,
was sitting straight again; I brought
the two hands up from underneath
the lid; they were stained from cigarettes
but otherwise clean, stone-dry and brittle.
I blew, and chemicals under my breath
rose, then fell, as dust might settle.

The hacksaw was out and into his wrist
that minute, rasping its way through flesh
as though it had been dry paper; the rest
was simple, snapping bones like chalk,
then whipping his hand off in a flash
and into a cushioned box; the right hand first
and then the left, the two laid flush,
wrapped over, and the lid jammed on.
We disappeared without needing to talk,
going our own ways, one by one,
taking with us the hands of Juan Peron.

Before we left I handed over a box
to the silent men who had stood behind me
watching, refining whatever their plans were,
too subtle to spot a simple hoax,
which is what I gave them. I'm holed up here
in this single room where they couldn't find me,
waiting until the right moment lands
like a dove with an idea in its beak
to put me in the money. So now, inside the Ark,
I'm left with the main chance, food for a week,
a telephone, and a clean pair of hands.

The Green, Grassy Slopes of the Boyne

Or, alternatively,
the Braniel housing estate.
The postman by the garden gate
hovers (except that, for me,
there is no gate, and the garden
is grass rubbed dead, and dog turds)
hovers, and tells me he's no postman
(I never catch the exact words,
maybe it's a park-warden).
At any rate, he makes it known
that he has come today
no, to deliver nothing. To send away.

But nothing changes here, or never has:
a few times snow
has covered the whole garden. When I show
him the photographs of myself
standing up fat and smiling
against that year's white-out,
all he can do is look away again.
I pull him back, show him
the whole extent of change
in a garden that, in any case,
was never his to cultivate,
winter or summer, one step beyond the gate.

That Friday, looking down
at a city greyed out by smoke
rising with its own sound,
thud after thud, and all the time
a choir of sirens
swooping to work, I was standing
right at the very centre of the garden
while indoors the radio
announced, interpreted, till its voice broke.
The sun set as it always does, lighting
the hills and burning up clouds like rags.
They were gathering the dead in plastic bags.

This time, again, he's leading me
up that same garden path
to a familiar height, where I can see
down years, without any photograph,
to myself and others marching, beating
hard toy drums and dragging past
The Green, Grassy Slopes of the Boyne.
When I come back
to the corner, I turn and start again.
The clouds are burning like photographs
all over again
and I turn around and go back, and around and back again.

The Third Day

My head is melting:
smears of hair and flesh-tone
are slipping through the fingers
of hands that are no longer
just so much skin and bone,
and return to where they'd risen

on my grandfather's palette
in some makeshift studio,
a damp back-parlour
in Belfast or Glasgow.
Now, while the paint's wet,
he'll turn the street corner

where my father might wait,
his hair shiny with Brylcreem,
to deliver another telegram
in Blitz-dark London:
sucking on a boiled sweet,
there's nothing he foresees

that could bring him any closer
to his young son, the grandson,
whose unborn arms and legs
will have grown away from him
like the head that's melting now
with ice cream and Easter eggs.

Sunday in Great Tew

8th November, 1987

1

It's time to get back to the car. Already, at half-past three,
the light's three-quarters gone, and back across the green
you can watch the shifting greys of a subtle fog by now
coming over to freeze the steps we leave, our ghosts' footprints,

to slight marks in November grass, and that's the last
of us this afternoon, this year, in this model village
a half-hour's drive from Oxford, where we come in summer
like the other tourists, to drink good beer, sniff woodsmoke,

and admire thatched roofs on sturdy, stone-built houses,
as though the whole place were a replica of some England,
an idea on show, unchanging, glassy, not quite touchable.
But this is November, and Sunday. It is Sunday in Great Tew.

2

Every visit nowadays is an act of remembrance,
measuring changes in us against some other summer
when we sat here drinking, and swapped our random gossip
– friends, work and books, hard politics or love –

across a wooden table in an always busy pub
with proper beer on tap, not the watery Oxford slops,
and where, as a speciality, they sell hand-made pipes,
briars and clay-pipes, every one the genuine article,

(though these, admittedly, we never got round to buying):
one year we're talking about that headstrong, happy girl
you'd chased unluckily for months; another, we're discussing
far-off acts of war, the real thing, here in the Falkland Arms.

3

The manor house, concealed behind thick trees and hedges,
might well be home now for some eccentric millionaire
who seldom shows his face; from the road going uphill
to the church, you can see through gaps to the house itself,

heavy and strong, like the brash history it suggests,
having and holding so much: was it here since the Civil War,
when the bookish man who owned the place, Lord Falkland,
was a loyalist who found himself outmanoeuvred?

Once he played patron here to the poet Abraham Cowley
– outmanoeuvred himself, in his way, by Parliament's
staunch worker Milton, true to different lights, but blind,
po-faced, pig-headed and holy, almost an Ulsterman.

4

Names of the wars change, and the protagonists change:
the church contains its various slabs of memorial stone
with names of the dead men, where today a single wreath
of poppies does its duty, pays them its stiff homage

of glaring red flowers for death, rootless and papery,
bunched together in grief or pride, or with indifference,
on a Sunday like any other Sunday in November;
there's a smell of damp mixed with that of genteel ladies,

and the cold slips forward from the walls and the dark floor
so that here, too, we must become aliens, shut out
from what we might be tempted to call ours, reminded
that the dead are close, that here the poppy is an English flower.

5

There are no words to find for the dead, and no gestures,
no sermons to be turned, no curses to lay now and for ever
on one house, or the other, or on both; no need
to rerun the scalding images they have left in our keeping,

or pitch hot misery into this cold comfort, as though
one ill-bred outburst here might make some sense of it;
there is no need to watch television in the afternoon
to understand that nobody has ever died with a good reason,

and say how the Irish slaughter one another like wogs;
there is no need, only now a blinding appetite,
this afternoon, tomorrow, the day after: in the Killyhevlin
Hotel the team from ITN will be ordering champagne.

6

One drink today, one pint of beer, and one short walk
in the sober afternoon around an English village,
a conversation jumping from one silence to another
in ripe Oxonian vowels, two figures on their own

in some pretend backwater with picture-postcard views,
slipping discreetly into a proper country churchyard
and quoting poetry, and laughing now that everything's
too late, imagining the right history for the place,

inglorious, largely mute: two generals discussing terms,
their fists set hard on the oak table that's between them,
where neither will say the word 'defeat', though both return
with different names for victory to their broken people.

7

Even in the middle of winter, the sky is everywhere,
folded above us as we walk with hands sunk in our pockets,
our fingers worrying over change and key-rings;
it covers us completely as a numbing anaesthetic

so that every time we might look up, the two of us,
the trees we can see with fog trailing in their branches,
the scarecrow standing up in its one blank field
(it looks from here like a scarecrow), the row of old houses

snug and expensive and empty, even the pub behind us,
all become incidental, oblique marks set in the margin,
swept out to the edges of a single clear perspective,
the one that matters most, or least, and never changes.

8

A flower of crumpled paper with its button of black plastic
has fallen from somebody's coat, and is lying here beside
a vacant phone-box opposite the village school,
along with a used packet of twenty Benson and Hedges

and what must be a bus-ticket; such modest litter
might be the last thing you notice, and for all the cars parked
there's nobody here but us walking out in the open,
and even we are making our way back to a car,

opening, closing doors, clicking in belts, switching on
dipped headlights and starting the engine; turning around
and taking a right at the deserted school,
on our way home, leaving absolutely nothing behind us.

ADAM'S DREAM

1996

The Situation

To speak exactly about the situation is difficult,
and yet to speak inexactly is unpardonable,
reshaping it at best as some half-blurred fable
where lines undraw themselves, boundaries move and halt,
the thing you see is never necessarily the thing
you see, and what happens there does not happen;
for the line undrawn draws the line, only to cheapen
what was dear-bought with its discreet bargaining.

Now the demand is that you deal with the situation
and come to the table with an answerable reply,
there is either warranted flatness or the clear lie
and between these, perhaps, a line kept at high tension
on which to balance or fall, a choice that draws you in
where there is no choice but to deal with the situation.

Meissen

Everything he touched, it fell to pieces:
small signs at first – the moth
whose wings just brushed his fingers
left them powdered with gold and silver,

with sharp dust scattered in a breath;
then the slightest pressure on a delicate page
would make it crumble, the least
gesture over a glass's edge

and the glass would cringe and crack.
Room by room, the house deformed
itself around him, the doors eased back
from their hinges, the wood split,

rafters and beams gave out and fell
to thick dust on dissolving carpets;
his hand, poised over the banister,
would have suddenly nothing to cling to,

and his bare head, like a clown's,
whitened under a shower of plaster.
Each fresh collapse would bring through
patches of sky, vistas of clear air,

emptiness surprising him everywhere
in failures and quick breakdowns.
When the house was almost gone,
its gables fizzling into the sky,

only the precious things were left:
the cabinets of good porcelain,
Derby, Sèvres, Limoges, Meissen,
somehow outlasting all the rest,

and their militant fragility
defeated him, defeated now
his heavy house, his body,
his heavy solid hands;

they left him without the grounds
for touching, with all his needs astray,
not ruined quite or hurt, but somehow
reduced, and better that way.

On a Good Day

The shadow over your shoulder
looks down, and you can't look down

from out on the very edge
where a cubic pressure of air

crushes or lifts maybe
even you

drunk and beat-up and weary,
still balanced, a heavy

head that rests on nothing
and will fall

from the edge of anything,
a displaced volume

of a certain weight
pressured, pressed

as shame, emblem,
sweet liquor

where the shadow looks
down, and you can't look.

Reno

At noon, in the building that has no daylight,
a rider steps into his wire globe
– above us by twenty or twenty-five feet –
and starts up a glittery motorcycle,

then a woman in sequins and little else
stands still at one point in his orbit,
untouched forever, as he drives up
and around the world on the wrong side.

Endtime

The flat road with no corners and no end
will take you further on, in either direction,
into the state of Texas; even at night
this is hot ground, it should be glowing red,
but instead the franchises are lighting your way,
part-empty, cool, just waiting you quietly
whenever you come, and you come sometime.

The woman who was sitting a table away
looks older than anything reasonable or possible,
and now she is here beside me
she has shaken my elbow and wakened me
before I am put to the question;
she moves up a jar of pickled jalapeños
and blesses me three times in the name of Jesus.

She will ask me three things, and she will wait
for no answers (the answers are there in my heart):
do I have eyes to see the manifest signs?
do I walk each day in fear of eternity?
– and then, as she leaves her shining table
to move on towards the night and the heat –
do I believe we are living in endtime?

Slumped on a low wall, out in the dark here
on the loud far edge of the parking-lot,
too tired for driving, too tired for anything,
you might as well be in on the secret;
you might as well be caught out on your own
with no questions and no answers,
finished, in Texas someplace, waiting dawn.

Breakfast

I cut and press the five blood oranges
into a jug, and sit down by the window.

Maybe the runners see me for a moment,
somewhere out on the very edge of attention,

as I sit drinking the blood of the oranges –
a table and a glass, a heavy head.

(This is the touch of hands that weigh and balance
like someone blind, who could feel colours once,

and sits at the window with a glass of blood.)

Bitter

If they had names once, their names are not to be spoken
without a shudder; if they had faces, their faces
are turned down now for good – forgotten, smeared things;
nothing is left to distinguish one from another,
a row of bared heads, heavy with disgrace and dishonour.
If there are words in which to remember their actions,
they will not form in the mouth, and a voice alone cannot bear them.

Exposed in sleep or drink, it may be that violence rises
as a sharp, sour taste in the throat, or a tension
winding through muscles until it reaches some point of abandon:
whatever it is takes shape in the dark, whatever
form or figure appears – some crouched, famished shadow
with plastery hair and the stretched lips of an enemy –
the hands and will together consent in strength to its murder.

A line of men, each of whom will have done nothing or something,
    stand with heads bowed before their accusers,
each of whom will speak bitterness, and use bitterness,
    until the hard tension passes, relief comes,
and at last the quiet shapes are laid to rest or abandoned.
    If there are victims, the victims are hard to distinguish
as taste from the tongue, the fist from the blow, or hands from the body.

The Brancusi Room

As he stares at the peeled head
of Brancusi's *Prometheus*
(exactly still, resting on nothing)
the gallery reels around him;
he becomes an unfixed point
in the white room
where all possible dreams of falling
confirm themselves,
taunted on the way down
by *Bird in Space*, its steadied leap
from here to there exactly.

It is afterwards, dizzied and shame-faced,
that his talk is of balance,
of precipices, chasms, headlong falls,
the leap of faith
involved in putting one foot out
in front of the other;
the story, to cap it all,
of the bicycle built for speed
he was given on his tenth birthday,
and which even now – look, look –
he cannot ride.

A Hard Place

Not everybody is happy, or loved:
despite that, at seven-thirty or thereabouts
this evening, some kids and some short-lived
breezes dawdled up here from the harbour,
all the way to the bar, and without
picking up, without placing an order
they left, slipped back into the heatwave
as if nobody had moved.

Even among the losing team
(heavy losers – one drinks, then cries some,
another mutters through old-time hymns
while his enemy half-sleeps on the table)
something comes loose, and maybe the rock seems
far enough from a hard place to let crumble,
like a sign slipping, or like some emblem:
an emblem of suffering and shame?

The Glen

There was a garden behind the labourers' cottage,
studded with white and blue, yellow and orange,
where waves of flowers and walls of trained roses
ran down a slope into grass, to the point
where shrubs and trim hedges marked a boundary;
beyond that, weeds and brambles, a tangle
of nettles and docken as the ground dropped
down finally into the glen. Trees spread over
the gap, and beneath them was darkness, the sound
of branches and leaves; sometimes, from underneath,
water invisibly going its own way.

So the boundary was a sheer edge, the slope a drop,
and the bright flowers had a shadow behind them
that could speak sometimes over brash colours
and mumble into the cottage's dry parlour
something fearful, or to do with sorrow,
a hard thing, extreme, just inches away
and unavoidable; no words, not an inch given,
but the glen still running behind everything,
always there at the end of a packed garden,
and me listening sometimes,
between us only the simple matter of falling.

The Creatures

At day's end, in a lull beneath stained and watery heavens,
  the beasts return in pairs to pace out the twilight
heavily, lightly: striped pigs, sad apes, the great lions,
  cattle and sheep, old bears, the hound and the badger,
creatures now without Adam to name or Noah to save them,
  coming back to a forest, a garden of calls and responses,
their eyes full of bleary light from skies full of water.

All around foliage moves in the air, making no progress
  this way or that; long vines, weighted branches
and outsized, flat leaves consort in wet tangles
  where birds rustle and screech, or where light animals
purposefully skelter, finding places to hide or to forage
  in a larger confusion of such ill-sorted species:
the coconut, the mangrove, the elm, the pine and the chestnut.

A red sun gutters here, as if at the point of exhaustion,
  from some far place, one beyond all purpose and action;
the moon comes; now insects flash up unknowable signals
  while lonely calls, like grief, go out in the darkness:
they echo each other, concluding that all has been done now,
  and all is to do again, for the creatures are leaving;
one by one, and with sorrow, they must enter the peaceable kingdom.

Peacetime

Half-way down you lose the sense of falling,
call off hostilities between things and the soul
and wave perhaps, now time is to spare,
on the clear road from here to wherever;
for everyone is crying in relief
and congratulation, historians and survivors
discuss their grievous memories on air,
dizzy in this late reprieve and freedom,
and it all hurts like a childbirth, crazy
with drugs and news and people and champagne.

This is all happening before its time
or after; this is weekend leave;
these are the experts and the blond children
ready to sing, like a happy army;
this is a good day for flying;
this is the cat's-
cradle of the bridge and the excellent sky;
this is the safe end of everything;
this is the beard and the dropping
smile of John Berryman going to heaven.

1990

Five Circumstances

1

There is a sad place, where everything is resolved.
The people smile there, but out of politeness,
and look forward to their time off-duty
which will not come. They consider this, also.

2

Having arrived at the point of utter exhaustion,
you must face the point of abandon, face up
to the point of despair, as to the last point
of land before the ocean: this is the point.

3

This is the man who has failed in everything
but wakes up happy to greet the world.
As the cat bounds into the filthy yard
he senses his good wishes being returned.

4

A packed room tenses as the conversation
holds up to wait for the decisive moment
when a man will announce in perfect English,
and with regret, that the conversations are ending.

5

It is like travelling with sorrow everywhere:
the business suit pressed but showing its age;
a newspaper folded in on the bad news;
a briefcase full of tears and pornography.

From the Porch

If you sat here long enough,
not any long time, but for lifetimes,
for the centuries without you,
then into your death and beyond it
in a moment, the space of a breath,
you would see just about everything:
colours on the sierras coming
and going, fires and black scars
for miles, then sudden regrowths,
years of pitiless summers
that beat this ground, snows freezing it,
all the generations of birds
circling and unidentifiable;
the passing hunters who squat
over worn stones, their voices
gone as you take a breath;
the hillsides opened by water,
the men who came for gold
and left without it, Chinese
workers camping out, soon gone,
and then, in the blink of an instant,
in half a breath, in less,
ourselves here watching and waiting
who are gone just as quickly,
to be followed it seems by everything:
noise and a blur of crowds,
then a sudden silence,
but one that's broken maybe,
like the quiet behind our sleep
when a dog nudges at the trash
or two cats scramble into each other,
and sounds start to rise and fall,
like breath at night coming and going,
of the tall horses moving uneasily
or deer that came in close at dusk,
the roosting birds, the sharp lizards,
the hare or the jack-rabbit
all following their noses,
like lost things.

An Eclipse

I walked home in the dark and beneath trees
that cried and scraped above me, as they strained
to keep themselves together in the wind;
a solid month of storms,
drunken calamities
that came to nothing, the weather on bad terms
with everyone, picking fights, ready to wound,
earnest of proper harm.

I walked back safe under the cracking branches
as fists of air pummelled and slapped me hard
for some good reason, as yet undeclared;
I felt glad and light-headed
to be in the clutches
of a gale that could break whole trees unaided,
yelling and stamping; head down, undeterred,
I tensed and decided.

I spoke across three thousand miles of weather,
drunk and exhausted, to you wide awake;
my closing time darkened your six o'clock
with half-unspoken anger
– a shadow, rather,
of something big, to be appeased like hunger,
beyond us, and on which we cannot look,
some close and awful stranger.

I woke up with the storm still in my head
and damage spread for acres, shattered wood
exposed and almost white across the road;
I sat on the cold stairs;
I ran and hid
to find myself naked, as if behind bars,
still grey with shadows, blurting out proud
sobs and baby tears.

I went outside tonight, again let loose,
where pieces of wood still clutter up the path,
to wait for the eclipse (for what that's worth –
a sight for lovers, who kiss
and cry in twos),
and standing on my own, watched the moon pass
into a coloured shadow of the earth,
pardoned, and numb with peace.

The Passions

Being obliged to climb higher, there is nothing else for it
but to try the steps, some solid, then one or two missing,
that cling to the inside wall; yet lichens and mosses

are at home on worn stones where, slippy with drizzle,
your feet slide and catch hold; one final scramble
and you are out in the open, the weather is loud and daylight

seems to come and go in gusts, brightening, darkening
that marginal road you drove along, the hills in the distance,
new farmhouses, and out on a rainy horizon, the sea.

Yet even here, high up in a far place, you are scarcely
alone – just look: all around, behind you and beneath you
there are the slow lines of raised, unreadable faces

which you must transform into figures expressing the passions
– rage, terror, pity, desire or ruinous sorrow –
and these are the very faces to see you through to the end,

all the way up, slipping and holding, climbing at last
to this platform half in ruins – a bridge or a tower,
but a bridge over nothing and a tower with no view from it –

until their perfect expressions are all wiped in an instant
and somebody – call it you – has to go down like a dummy
and measure an empty distance between here and the ground.

Delaval

Here is Mr Dillyval, and a charming set of Glasses that sing like nightingales, and we have concerts every other night.

Thomas Gray, to William Mason, 1761

Alone, where there is no etiquette to breach,
the hands may go free to toy with a napkin,
dismember gutted fruits, or wet the fingers
and edge them over one particular glass

until a note starts up and holds briefly,
clear, then fitful and guttering. May a note gutter?
It is later than midnight in the depleted Parlour,
yet the reflexes of taste still prick like nerves,

as if conscience would speak on behalf of decorum
and ask repentance for our every mistake
in the name of such fitness. At the sounded note
one flame does gutter; it is time indeed

to snuff the candles and leave the room to darkness.

⋆

How meagre the skill one has in such music!
How halting and imperfect, how much like a failure
seems even the recollection of Mr Dillyval
and his concerts *impromptu* on the musical glasses

that haunt the same room now, however faintly.
All evening, seated next to the contrivance,
he played, touching harmonics from the vessels
arranged by diameter, and for each note a colour,

melodies at an even pace, bright with echoes
that rang and repeated and circled themselves,
returning always to the placed intervals.
Often that season the company sat late

when there was much talk, and not without wit,
over the music or the manner of it,
ingenious improvements to the mechanism
or the fit posture from which to touch the colours.

Although not wholly wasted on the air,
such sounds do not return, and a bell strikes
to mark the quarter-hour, just once.
The blood comes back to its slow course

and customary rhythms gather ground,
not troubled far by virtuosity,
nor shaken greatly by such memories
when the melodies themselves are past recall.

(Here is a small failure, and no consequence,
safe in the dark alone, returning homeward
on the familiar, unmistaken path
upstairs, the weary way.)

On Show

There is, first, the disappointment of a case
around even this insured figurine:
you will stare for minutes, and more the next day,
until your sad amazement has grown routine,
at the face and the small body in porcelain,
her eyes that look through glass
as though towards you, to confirm beautifully
and for good the usual futilities:
the projects for love, like plans for money or knowledge,
shut away in a clear light, all of them frangible.

The Glass Harmonica

Now it starts:
the music being played on glasses,
'unearthly', echoing itself, up in the air,
dividing into separate, ringing parts
that make feints and passes
at each other like a courting pair
alone, together, alone,
sounding the resonance of one another's hearts.

(But of this world all along:
that these had grown
above themselves, were wrong
and overblown
parts of a voiceless song,
is easily shown.)

Like a tulip-bud
the smallest glass, the highest note,
is lead-painted with the rest in its own shade,
and of all the *virtuosi* in the flood
of players who had by rote
each composition, the last has played
his last, and waits alone
in quiet now, with all the music in his blood.

About Lisbon

Now the city is almost completely empty,
the night is far through, with no moon, just stars;
a dog maybe scrambles in and out of the rubbish
along a side-street of no real interest or merit:
it's as if the whole place is ready to be erased
and somehow somebody has told the inhabitants.
Late as it is, there ought surely to be people
to find their way around the city of Lisbon
and guide me, who am not here, to the very spot

where the public clock stopped on a Sunday
and the tremors began. Is it perhaps because
that morning has yet to come, or because
the catastrophe has been too long forgotten
that nobody speaks, that there is nobody to speak,
that I must wander for hours an unknown city
and there is nobody here to ask the time?

The Earthquake

A row of figures on the mantel, not yet of any particular value,
begin to tremble and burr, edging their way to the edge.

Scintillant dusk: outside, an unmistakable hue and commotion
of falling things, panic; after-the-fact calls of alarm.

The shepherdess has just taken the plunge with her pastoral lover
and gone off into shards and smithers, to smithereens.

Academic Sentences

1
First Principles

This cannot be seen, and accordingly
it is incapable
of producing the image you claim
to see; it cannot be heard, in any
useful or commonly acceptable
sense of the term,
and so can hardly emit those sounds
you find so troubling; it cannot sustain
itself on anything other
than the thin
air of your imagination: you must
allow it therefore to die.

All of the buildings are empty, all
of the men and women
have left them,
and what remains
is the focus principally
for objective interest, for the sorting
and weighing of evidence; not certainly
for your hurt brooding, with its
intrusions of desire and exaggeration
(both, frankly, vain and ridiculous),
or the interruptions
of insignificant deaths.

A grand project
for nothing; visions, plans,
lost patterns; two worlds
of life and death, involved
only in an image of something
invisible: none of this
counts, in the place
where somehow you must
build solid structures
on soft ground, whatever you choose
to understand by the word
for clay, or reddened earth.

2
Point A

She lives now in an unbuilt
project of the brothers Adam,
among purely notional
fitments and decorative schemes,
prepared, at any
and every moment, to
go public with this odd
address, this mausoleum,
to christen it Point A
and perhaps, should it prove

necessary, herself sell
tickets at the door.

Even with its glories on show,
certain secrecies
involved in the building
will probably remain
obscure: tiny letters, from Alpha
to Omega, worked into the stones
of the main staircase; arcane
patterns on the tiles inside
one particular fireplace; a frieze
high over the entrance
bearing signs
of the sun and stars.

Her eye for detail is
exact and terrifying,
involving as it does
the recognition of thousands
of points of error
or of neglect, architectural white
lies accepted in the course of things
but which, if she comes
into the house, she must
put right, moving
from room to room
and restoring all she finds.

3
Eidolon

I am not speaking
at all now, although I am
surrounded as I sit here
by moving blocks
of silence and bad sound; there are lights
and noises that make their way
to me from the night outside,

and there is my own
slumped figure reflected, facing me
but with the fast lights
inside it, spread
across the window.

I would ask things
of this image, I would
interrogate it with an impressive
thoroughness and integrity, if
there were a possibility
of its answering my questions;
the image would reply
– candidly, shamefully, stricken –
if there were really a chance
of my questioning it aloud:
but neither I nor the image
must speak a syllable here.

The image is a shadow with features;
my features are shadowed
horribly over its face, the clear
surfaces and the parts that recede
into darkness: pierced
by roadlamps and headlights,
the likeness ghosts itself,
it negotiates
helplessly between two
sleeping partners, between
the heat of bodies
and the kindcold sky.

4
Walking in the Garden

Although the ground
is level and the path clear,
I could be walking a wire
as I speak to her,
beginning to fall in one
direction and then beginning
to fall in another,
teetering steadily,
balanced and terrified, talking
about nothing at all
with my head
straight up and looking forwards.

As she turns off
the marked path, towards
the slab
of architecture and the black
open doorway that leads
straight into its heart,
I call her back
on some pretext, seeing
already a prospect of ruins,
vistas of pure waste,
unpeopled wreckage,
Babylon, dust.

And she answers, but what she says
is unbearable,
it cannot be faced
and has to be forgotten; she
fills my shadow
and moves from A to B,
from B to A, speaking about
choices beyond my making,
touching the laden apple-
tree and laughing, whether at me
or herself it is
impossible to tell.

5
Point B

After so many drawings,
so many outlines
sketched in pencil, scrubbed
and redrawn, and later whole designs
inked meticulously
on sheets of heavy paper, after
so many walls and windows, porticos
and pilasters appearing, shifting,
vanishing sometimes,
after all these exertions, these artful
comings and goings, the mind
and the hand rested together.

The grand project (B, for ease
of reference) exists therefore
(if 'exists' is the appropriate word)
in multiple states, some of them
conjectural, its development
and interruptions, the conceptual
leaps and the digressions
hard to distinguish, just as it is
debatable, finally,
whether the building
is located in imagination
or in memory.

(False starts and premature endings,
losses and conjectures, someone
listening
to a piano with her face turned
always half away,
deep in a house
where all the doors are closed,
a figure remembered or
imagined, but subtracted,
its name
going in the fire, and now
scorched almost away.)

Adam's Dream

It was the first morning after the earthquake:
imagine, Jamie, that prospect of desolation!
Everywhere, figures such as mine were moving
like ants among remnants of pointless mazes,
dodging fires that burned on in the daylight
and structures liable still to collapse about them,
though searching really for the dead, one supposes,
the thousands of souls buried all together
in Lisbon that Sunday morning. I am not idle,
Jamie, even in the few sultry hours
of sleep allowed me by this Roman weather,
and as I dreamed of the Portuguese disaster
I was starting to discern, in those very ruins,
the bold lines and the curves, the sweeps and contours
of a city to replace the shaken quarters,
laid out by me, and plotted in each detail
to accord with precept, principle, and good practice
in the antique taste which I have so well mastered
and of which you are, I know, an eager student.
(Of course, no more than you have I seen Lisbon,
but given such accounts of the devastation
it seems the place is fairly a *tabula rasa*
for a fellow of gifts and genius to work on.)

Think of it, to raise the Adamitic city!
I have listened to the invaluable Clérisseau
as he tutors me in figures of a morning,
repeating Voltaire's wisdom on the subject,
that Providence is under grave suspicion
for allowing such catastrophes to happen:
nonsense, the thing is plainly Heaven's judgement
intended for my behalf – do not you see it?
And the city to replace that shattered Lisbon
will be a wonder to the world of the discerning,
displaying to all Europe one true fashion
of the best taste, and flights of studied daring,
to trumpet my resource, my infinite merit,

and so become the first of Adam's cities.
Who knows, Jamie, but that you might be my partner
in building even London from its ruins?

As much as skill, good offices are needed
from men of rank whose tastes we must encourage,
as best we can these days, with good example
and now and again, of course, judicious puffing:
one may not win that merited preferment
without a word or two in the right quarters,
and even here in Rome I have been active
in winning the good esteem of noble patrons
(not patrons yet, but like to be for someone),
and I take care that my name spreads through the city
as a likely man for great things in the future.

You recall I have written before of Piranesi
whose work bearing the handsome dedication
you will have received by now in a fine binding,
Antichità Romane, the Roman matter
put over with great art, and greater detail
– which gives you, Jamie, solid ground for study.
This Piranesi is known to sing my praises
where weight is given to his good opinion,
so I have ample reason to be hopeful.
To see the antique world as you should see it,
ruined, but with the ruins free of clutter,
exposed as an ordered prospect of grand damage,
with here and there inconsequential figures
caught still as they go scuttling through the columns
is just what Piranesi seems to manage
in those etchings that have been my constant wonder
since I came here to Rome, this half-empty city.

In fact, it was the *Antichità* in folio
which featured in my dream about the earthquake:
not just the labyrinths of brick and *tufa*
half-grown with weeds, or the great dark masses
of drops and shadows, walls going on forever,
which I transposed from Rome into old Lisbon,

but the books themselves, the four bound volumes
which, you remember, Bute had desired of me
all of three months ago. Now, the bold Scipio
– without so much as a gesture of acquaintance,
a casual word of favour or approbation,
which would count for much, and very well repay me –
has sent the volumes back with a cold *Thank you*,
as though I might have furnished them on approval
for his Lordship like a humble bookseller,
not a free Scot of generous means, and genius!
I shall be revenged on Bute, one way or other,
perhaps exactly as last night I dreamt it:
at Kensington, I'll wait for him on the bridge there,
while his barge progresses slowly down the river,
with him and *Madame la Princesse* busy as usual,
the Princess of Wales and her First Minister
stewing together through an English summer
(and causing the vessel some distress already
by their exertions, it being far from sturdy).
Under the bridge they'll come, like two locked wrestlers,
for me to let drop all four hefty volumes
on to the brilliant couple *in flagrante*
as they pass under the yoke & Robt. Adam,
then send them down into the dirty water:
I'll fell Bute dead with the same Piranesi.

When Clérisseau arrived this morning, bedraggled,
(where had he lodged, I wonder? had he slept even?)
I put figures aside, and openly spoke with him
of the earthquake, of the plans of the Almighty,
of Piranesi, darkness, and Bute's exposed *derrière*.
We agreed this was a dream of injured merit,
a portent maybe, though confused and inscrutable,
of the great things we may expect in this world:
is it to be our lot, however deserving,
to be shadowed always, to be accidental figures
among the intransigeant, huge forms?

Jamie,
I believe the heat of Rome may bring me fevers

for which no remedy exists but work,
so commending that to you, in very good spirits
(at the door is news of another invitation),
I return now to take up my graceful labours.

De Gustibus

A bitter taste, and the tongue constrained always in the mouth;
candles at midday; a Scottish damp and the reek of mildew;
a painted room blistered and spoiled; the pattering of a moth
all day confronting smeary panes of the same window;
baronial vistas of unworked and waterlogged ground
into which the house itself begins surely to subside;
locked out of the way, plate tarnishing to the sound
of scraped, raw voices: soon all will have to be denied.

Beyond this, an entire geography of ruin,
of ancient things brought down and broken to fragments,
restructures silently the half-darkness and rain
to clear and balanced forms; a light from the south brings
hope to the woodwormy desk, the card table in segments,
cracked delftware, the brutish glass and inkstand: tasteless things.

The Authorities

It is true: knowledge is indeed matter for advancement
(Robert alone one morning with a volume of antiquities),
and principles of taste well founded on those sureties
from ancient practice will not lack proper emolument.
For each design one can imagine some enhancement,
but to rid the outlines of whatever superfluities,
to chasten style in a stern purging of impurities,
will expose the essential form, a severe monument.

Yet the monumental alone will not answer to taste:
one must make account first for domestic fashion
that endures for the moment, light fluency and grace,
gaiety even – not the under-message of the authorities
(think of Spalato, the huge palace of Diocletian,
like all Dalmatia falling continually into ruin).

A Pause

We are close now, it may be, to the delicate matter
which requires to be touched gently if touched upon,
and for which all reserves of forethought and compassion
must lie ready to hand; neither to hurt nor flatter,
neither to let pass falsehoods nor to dissimulate,
and yet allow the substance to make itself apparent –
these are the special tactics of reserve and restraint
for which, and in which, patience is (so to speak) infinite.

The hesitation must arise from discomfort, even from pain,
a pause both taken and given; what will then emerge
may not in all decency be spoken of as yet,
although you may infer that its outline is sufficiently plain:
the imagination has enough here upon which to enlarge
in a quiet moment, and with such tact as it sees fit.

The Rival

It is not genius at all: rather, a certain facility
conjoined with application, and with luck perhaps,
which takes him far, striking the occasional felicity
in the course of things, but not daring to lapse
from the dull idiom for which he is praised so,
each project merely a serviceable facsimile
of something genuine, not his, and long ago
perfected, but refined now to a lucrative futility.

This is not complaint, but philosophy: if his public is deluded
in applauding and rewarding him, little is proven;
one's own merit, infinite merit, might be given
hot praise as readily as indifference or blame,
and still it would remain to amend the taste of the time
regardless of all – promise, eminence, genius included.

The Dedication

When Piranesi scrubbed the plate clean of its dedication
(to whom, out of discretion, let us not specify),
it was not towards any *milord* of the English nation
that *Roman Antiquities* now cast a flattering eye
but to ROBERT ADAM, ARCHITECT, the inscription
entered there like proper Latin, its own antiquity
amply attested by the cracked and weathered stone
on which the master spelt out his new dedicatee.

Robert's name, imagined in a garden of worn granite,
is therefore at once novel and enormously aged,
an artist's name preserved on the work of an artisan
(and all of this itself art, a graceful conceit),
so that nothing is old, or new, entirely: thus privileged,
he is heir to the name and title of an ENGLISHMAN.

In the Sketchbook

Page upon page of the abandoned and the lost,
ideas without commission, flourishes, or gestures simply;
they crowd in from nowhere as if to build a new city
which is always beginning and cannot ever be finished,
for the first line drawn already imagines its parallel,
its perpendicular supports, and then embellishments,
the patterns that may be summoned in an instant,
accepted or rejected, found wanting or judged well.

This city is, naturally, without any inhabitants:
there is no room, and besides the dangers are great;
they will not suffer when finally the buildings are razed,
when the flat facades and the disproportioned pediments
crease and collapse into each other, and the crazed
architecture folds compactly into the stuff of light.

The Aftermath

One by one, without show, and almost meticulously,
from underneath the splintered and multicoloured rubble
everybody emerged, all of the broken and innocent dead,
into a morning hazy with mizzle and lingering smoke
to dust themselves down and take stock of the catastrophe,
adrift suddenly in this new architecture of chaos
but able to recognise each other beneath masks of ash
and tear-lines, with open astounded eyes, bewildered
by movement again, the turns and surprises of their raised bodies.

In His Place

Maps on tables are charts of losses, ruin;
plotting vistas no longer there, he stumbles
over mazes of stone and marble turned to
pebbles, marks in the ground, sand, scrubby grasses.
Nearly finished, he sees the city rising
clear in front of his body, holding steady,
almost tangible, moving, breathing even,
so that stone is not stone, but white and fleshy
tissue, beaten and dense with living substance.
Carried out of such places, he imagines
cities bodied in airy, cold perspectives,
sees himself for a second their dim figment
raised in error among the classic orders,
figured simply for scale between the buildings.

Lines on the Demolition of the Adelphi, *1937*

Reader, I am the ghost of Robert Adam
Come from the Purgatory of the proud
To a London of headlights, fumes, and tarmacadam
Where these old buildings have been disallowed

As fusty relics in the way of things,
To watch the Terrace fall, and wince again
While down the curious equipment brings
Investments once already down the drain

(Though now, indeed, the losses are not mine,
And I have pains other than injured pride
To see me through the ruins, for no design
Gives comfort in the place where I abide),

Yet I discern beneath the sooty dust,
Nothing of lasting worth, no second Rome,
Merely an English place, mean, gone to rust,
Not after all the imagination's home,

And built on little more than unpaid debts,
Its future mortgaged and its past resigned,
No better than where Piranesi sweats
Beside me, in the prison he designed.

PASTORALS

2004

Ποιμενίαν ἄγλωσσος ἀν᾽ ὀργάδα μέλπεται ᾿Αχὼ
    ἀντίθρουν πτανοῖς ὑστερόφωνον ὄπα.

An echo is when sound comes back late, and misses itself,
with no tongue to call its own: in deep pasture-land
birdsong is repeating when the birds themselves have flown
out of earshot – have flown straight into the daylight
of broad fields, echoless, where voices leave on the wind.

Two Trees

Weeds upon weeds, sticky with cables and jags,
made the path I was on hardly a path at all,
more a net of stalks and shoots, zig-zags
slowing my pace right down to a crawl
as I picked my way, if way you could call
it, half that morning in a drenched glare
after the hound, and its nose-down, long-haul
trek on some urgent but obscure affair
still far from over, and in which I had some share.

Blue dragonflies were switched on by the sun
and clattered into action; warily
I cleared the obstacles one by one,
but knew I was lost; all eyes were on me
(I didn't doubt for a moment they would see),
and what had felt like silence an hour ago
had turned now to a full cacophony
of things conferring, scuttling, in the know:
an audience perhaps, intent on this one show.

I came to a cleared hollow, where two trees
stood off from one another, bright with moss
that covered them like fur or a disease;
some rain was falling now, while just across
from where the trees put on a greenish gloss
as water caught in drops on their long hair,
I saw myself waiting and at a loss
for where to go, or whether I should dare
the wrong way out; the hound was neither here nor there.

So I stayed alone, at the far end of my luck,
searching the daylight for a way to go,
the path to one side, on the other the stuck
souls of Fraelissa and Fradubio
confirmed in bark and moss, always to grow
apart in separately wordless pain,
able only to move in the wind, with no
eyes to cry out, and just the good rain
for tears, not once to touch each other ever again.

The Cup

All around the lip, twisting and winding, tendrils of ivy
have stretched over themselves, with clusters of yellow berries
picked out hard and minute in the sculpted wood.
A girl is leaning underneath; she is not of this world
by the look of her, one hand holding the hem of her dress,
the other toying with a gemstone between her breasts,

while on either side of her, two big men stand glaring
at each other, having their say with faces full of bile,
and taking turns with dirty looks and bitter words
to which she is all but oblivious; she smiles slightly
as she looks at the one, then she looks at the other smiling,
while they go at it hammer and tongs, both in love with her:
the sad truth shows in their sore and haunted eyes.

Next to these, you can see an old codger perched on a rock,
a fisherman with his net, stripped here to the waist,
and ready to make a cast far out over the water
so that he seems to balance back and aim with all his strength
like a man half his age; on his neck the veins and sinews
are drawing tight as he concentrates, steadies himself,
and remembers only his body, which is no longer old.

Beside him, far away, is a boy who couldn't care less,
watching (*not* watching, in fact) the vineyard terraces
near harvest-time; as he drapes himself over a wall of stones
a pair of foxes get down to work, one making light
of his breakfast, the other snatching bunch after bunch of grapes,
and all this time the little guy works and works, taken up
entirely with a fragile, half-finished wicker cage
he'll use as a trap for crickets, and their prison,
plaiting and turning the stalks, snapping them, starting again.

Below this, pointy acanthus gathers and multiplies,
and the base of the cup is leaves, then leaves upon leaves.

Theocritus

A Gloss

Running like that, his arm in hers,
two wobbly penstrokes, characters

against a wall in streetlit rain,
they make a word I can't explain

or dare not, as they pelt away
from us, and what we hardly say,

towards some obscure privacy

(for sleep or sorrow, anger, sex?)
maintaining their mysterious checks

and balances, impossibly.

Visitors

The little girl who meets me in the tomb
and asks for *caramela, caramela,*
can hardly make me out, and in no time
when I am gone, she will no longer tell
one boiled sweet from another people give
her in the musty shadows, casting shadows
into this echoing, used-out grave
where every day they gather, and she follows.

As I step out from the dead dark to the sun
I meet a line of uncles, visitors
in hats and coats, their shadows all but gone,
who leave me with my hands full, looking down
the red-tiled hall under high concrete stairs,
and say goodbye with sweeties and half-crowns.

At Castlereagh Church

The sun goes out in pink and purple
late on a late Easter Sunday,
while at the gates a courting couple
begin to take their winding way
from church down towards Gilnahirk,
through whin-blossom and blackcurrant
along the hedgerows where they walk:
primroses, docken and wild mint.

My father in his travelling clothes,
my mother in her summer coat:
they feel the chill, and walk in close
to each other on a dropping road
past fields and gardens, weeks before
the clematis will risk a flower.

Pastoral

Spring this week came breezing in
early, unconsidered, rash,
fighting where it could not win
no-colours of earth and ash

only with the frailest things:
blossom holding itself tight,
crocuses with folded wings
glancing flame, a change in light

switching bare trees into life
morning after morning, though
frost may come yet like a knife
late, and there may be late snow

coming from somewhere even now.
Wakened early, in the dark,
miles from you, I saw a bough
flare with buds, and make its mark

over against the odds; I saw
everything half-edged with fire
when both heart and eyes are raw:
nothing shaped, nothing entire.

You, I know, were late to bed
while I paused to let the day
make good what I might have said
with whatever I might say.

The Scald

Half-way up, on the inside, here,
of my right forearm, is the scald:
a whitish outline like a mended tear
in skin that is thirty years healed
– or more than thirty, as it must be –
and was my wrist, the time I scaled
the kitchen table, when a pot of tea
came down; the burn smacked first, then held

and held on while the heat pressed hard
but where, now, you can touch, and touch again,
where you can push into the soft skin
and put your finger on this pucker-scarred
ragged circle the size, say, of a coin,
then take your lips and touch them to the scald.

Air and Angels

The road might as well be made from sun and water,
the way it has shimmered and glared this half-hour
as it snakes along from here to there;
and it would lead you on, if you'd a mind
to go – three parts mirage, something
and nothing, light for the sunblind –
until I lost you in the flash and flare
with everything close, but miles off; tricks and lies
in what you see: all hit and miss,
for a cloud comes, as it will, and
the light changes anyway in a second
to leave those little flares behind your eyes
that play through shadows and faces, just like this.

Not that those shapes are ghosts, and not that
my eyes can't remember things, or tell them apart;
not that the dazzle or glitter ever falls flat;
but it glints back from however far ahead
you've gone – the hint, the something astray
and unsaid for too long, then better not said.
So we end up without a place to start,
all things being equal, with just such
disparity as the road or the weather gives
the two of us, always this far away;
or the sunlight makes you frown, in spits and spats
of rain that come to nothing, just
seeming to kiss your eyes for a second, and no more than that.

Work: 1958

Hardly another car on the whole road
to Cookstown from the far end of Tyrone;
hardly another traveller in town,
but shopkeepers and farmers by the cartload

in the Royal Hotel, piled up at a bar
so busy now, so packed, that there's barely
room to lean across, or to catch the ear
of a customer among this crowd in early

for the weekend, scarcely time to catch the eye
of a barman working himself off his feet;
matches, and just one goodwill round to buy,
then back to the lodging house in Union Street,

where scarcely a word passes, as you sit
down to a tea of half-stale soda farls
and eggs fried hard: at last a cigarette,
then your letter home, to 17, Mount Charles,

from which address, six months or more ago,
you buried your father, a private, estranged man
you hardly knew, and now will never know.
Packing up samples outside in the van,

you wonder where this leads, and where it ends:
a cold March night washed up in Cookstown;
saddlery and leather; an uncle who sends
you everywhere but home; and the road down

towards forty, blind and narrow with the grime
and smoke you breathe in, sharp as the night air –
but you know all the roads, the time served there:
the boredom and the sorrow and the time.

Foreknowledge

That nothing comes or goes at this hour,
when poems are ticking over in the dark
and everything here is the same colour,
long before dawn's handiwork
can begin to show or tell
or count for much, if it will count at all.

Maybe then, with plenty to admire,
– the room assembling itself, her face
familiar again, as the same face –
the day will come in, brisk and spruce,
sure of itself, with energy to spare
and time to burn. This hurts; it will hurt more.

The Victory Weekend

May 1945/ May 1995

Friday

At six, we went to drink beer on the roof:
   we hoisted ourselves up the dusty steps
that gave straight on to slates, and sat aloof
   from London, with its parapets and rooftops

stretching away in straight lines everywhere,
   on level terms now with the moving trees
that stood together hugely in the square,
   then balanced tumblers gently on our knees

so that, while all around us still there rose
   the last of Friday's heat, now we would pass
a half-hour until dusk in hunched repose,
   cold light between our fingers and cold glass

like talismans, or prizes lately won,
  tokens of lead and water turned to gold
and turned to catch the sun, full of the sun;
  their wink and glint ours now to have and hold.

The glasses empty, we edged back again
  to switch on lights, and change, then wander down
to streets that were still warm, with lane on lane
  of buses and hot cars all set for town

but nudging forward only by degrees,
  while we half-ran ahead, still hand in hand,
keeping our balance with a certain ease,
  or flying, really, not needing to land;

we leaned into each other as we turned
  tight corners of short cuts, and rattled past
tourists in lines, the beggars that they spurned
  and we left standing, getting there at last

a minute or two early, out of breath,
  then up more staircases, against the odds
to beat the curtain and perch just beneath
  the high roof on our cheap seats in the gods.

That night King Arthur and his Britons made
  their stand against the entire Saxon race,
Woden and all those other gods of the shade
  who hid in woods and caves, in every dark place,

a standing army of warlocks, spirits, nymphs
  emerging naked from enchanted streams
where they might tempt the hero with a glimpse
  of breasts in half-light, haunt him down in dreams,

then drag him to his ruin in the mere;
  the forest trees were something more than trees:
one nick, and they might cry aloud for fear
  or anguish, one false note and they would seize

a man and send him reeling through the air;
   while music zoomed and buzzed and sang up high
bad spirits and good, that flitted everywhere,
   parleyed and fought across a painted sky.

After his unsurprising victory
   brought the land back to Arthur mile by mile,
from cliffs far over the delighted sea
   out came at last the Spirit of the Isle

who sang to Purcell's music Dryden's words,
   a rising measure for the planets above,
and swept on inland, to the flocks and herds
   at peace in the seat of pleasure and of love,

in time with pastoral, a new-blooded nation
   ready to stretch now into its great year
with harmony and thunder, jubilation,
   and minds serene and calm and free from fear.

We left there, jittery with spectacle
   and full of music, at the music's speed;
London transfigured, half a miracle,
   but half something expected, took the lead

and steered us both, in giddy loops, zig-zags,
   to the flat, to bed, and through the panoply
of streets packed out with foreigners and flags
   in a city all dressed up for victory.

Saturday

Wellington, Blenheim, Spitfire, Hurricane:
   the name for each familiar silhouette,
labouring like a model aeroplane
   up there in thin formation, was pre-set

in what I learned, like most boys of my age,
   from war-comics, from films on TV,
when fighting men would slash the screen and page
   with blinding fire, or screams of agony –

exotic cries from Germans or Japanese
   at the extremities of pain and fear
were more grist to the mill: we took up these
   in playgrounds where the War went on all year,

when stockpiled arms were both elaborate
   and fiercely imagined, every shell
had its right calibre, all accurate
   as little pedants moved in for the kill.

Knowing their names, I pored over the sky,
   and as the planes kept up their stately pace
I stood in close to you, watching them fly
   over us and away, until no trace

was left in clouds or the resounding air
   of shapes familiar fifty years ago,
engines once listened out for everywhere,
   a drum and buzz distinct from the known, low

thrumming of German bombers on the nights
   when London took a pasting and took fire,
cascades of bombs setting its heart alight
   to leave it by daytime a smouldering pyre

with figures like stick-figures in attendance
   – fire hoses and tin helmets, stretcher-men
to bear away the dead with routine patience,
   black tons of rubble, miles of rot and ruin –

then life resuming stubbornly all around
   with boredom and endurance hedging bets
on who would win the day, and the days drowned
   in weak beer, wrapped in smoke from cigarettes.

When I was born, the whole show had been over
   for seventeen years; a new and stilted war
was being played behind-hand, under cover,
   with solid counters ready everywhere:

Castro and Kennedy, the Bay of Pigs;
   Berlin smashed and possessed and cut in two:
prowled over by B-52s and MIGs,
   Europe was scarcely likely to pull through,

so the last War went into storybooks,
   and boys pretending to be soldiers crept
up on each other, while jumpily in nooks
   and crannies all the stealthy missiles slept

their way through a strange peacetime, and through whole
   decades of stand-off, bluff, and false alarm,
as I slogged out the long campaign through school
   and won it, having come to no real harm.

Now you and I watched ribbons dip and swag
   where fast jets smashed and screamed over the Mall,
spreading the colours of the Union Flag
   behind them in a single billowy trail

that seemed to be taken up all through the crowd –
   those hats and t-shirts in red, white, and blue,
the streamers and the shell-suits, those pale, proud
   faces of a belated, happy few

in thousands upon thousands, in one place,
   as if the War was ending for the first time
here and today, as if the closest race
   was won, and peace was novel and sublime

as food or beer or sunshine or deep sleep
   to men starved and exhausted and worked dumb
who know for now the prize is theirs to keep,
   the day of execution will not come.

All fantasy: their fantasies; my own;
  the show an exercise in make-believe
disguised as memory; all the overblown
  music and glitter of a coarse, naive

history-carnival with its royalty
  and TV cameras, but no catch of pain;
cheap victory; boozy fellowship; a free
  people forgetting everything again

in a rush, as flags wave and the songs are sung
  just like before, but nothing like before:
something was wrong, or I was in the wrong
  place, but I needed to hear and see no more,

I don't know why. That day, we walked for miles
  out through the celebrations and away
to an empty City, the Barbican, St Giles
  dwarfed there in Cripplegate, its stones awry

and built over with brick, since the bombs burst
  everything open, scattering the bones
of Milton and John Foxe with fire and tempest
  where now only the blind sunlight bore down.

We walked up Moorgate then to Bunhill Fields,
  alone with a hundred thousand of the dead
jumbled beneath our feet, where old ground yields
  nothing – not an inch – to the heaviest tread,

the same hard earth where, packed away, the crazed
  bones of William Blake are lying deep
and sightless in oblivion, unraised
  for ever in unmarked and boundless sleep,

so steady they were not shaken by the bombs
  those years ago, so set and straitly laid
that they will be secure, whatever comes
  to blast or blitz the city where they hide

in the long nonsense of futurity
when memory will forget itself, let go,
and leave the dead to their conspiracy
of quietness, mute echo, afterglow.

Tired out, we dawdled back towards the crowds
on holiday, like us, while the May sun
cast from behind a pinkish stream of clouds
its sharp, indifferent light on everyone.

Sunday

The narrow and wide streets were trodden grass
between marquees and stages in Hyde Park
as you and I edged slowly through the mass
of trippers who had chosen to embark,

like us, for the improvised and busy town
islanded here in green, where stalls and tents
stood in straight ranks, good servants of the Crown,
for veterans in their different regiments

who gathered like so many new recruits,
waiting for something – for unlikely showers,
with their umbrellas, blazers and lounge-suits
slightly too large; for tea at all hours,

or for a known face to approach and speak
in a familiar language some good word
to make sense in the hubbub, however weak
that voice, or however poorly it was heard.

Their Sunday glances searched and drew a blank,
for we were on our way home, by midday,
and hurried on, giving neither name nor rank,
against the crowd's flow, two specks in its way,

to find ourselves on time for the train back
    to Bristol, riding westward on our own
(or nearly) down the miles of Brunel's track
    away from the weekend, away from London,

and landed before long in our attic space
    that looked straight into clouds over the Downs,
where we and the great elms sat face to face
    with ringdoves, finches, rooks in their black gowns,

where a purlin squeaked and scraked in gusts of wind
    and rooftiles thrummed through days and nights of rain,
but where now only thin shadows inclined
    across the carpet, as every windowpane

fielded a sky full of the sun, a glare
    in which the birds were tiny shadows, strafed
with light, while through that blanket fire the blare
    of high coarse voices as they chased and chafed

– seagulls in raiding-parties from the coast –
    haunted the air, became the daylight's sound,
but an all-clear too, a sign we had not lost,
    sharp and intact, re-echoing all around.

Wrapped up in peace, I was nearly twelve years old,
    waiting for school to finish for the day:
rain in the light, the weather turning cold,
    traffic outside with traffic in its way

not moving, locked on the Stranmillis Road,
    on the Malone and Lisburn Roads, stacked down
to Shaftesbury Square, or where some episode
    or other must have closed the heart of town,

and taking it for granted, thinking past
    diversions and stopped buses, through road-blocks
and windows strapped with tape against the blast
    of bombs not yet exploded, or the shocks

that glass was heir to; I would sit and wait
for twenty to four, the bell, and day-release,
the slow trek across town to be home late,
through desolation with the name of peace,

a burst map of the past, claims and admissions,
abstracted history cracked up, falling in
with the blown brick and concrete, dull attritions
of a war I didn't start and couldn't win.

The burn of sunset now, two decades on,
lit miles of sky in coral and louder red:
I was safe; the past was over; the sun shone
pitilessly on me and all the dead,

for this was pastoral; I could almost see
the dead together in a wall of light,
closing their hearts, climbing away from me,
into a ghost-glare early in the night,

in march-past, in a simple, strict parade,
until the fireworks split up in the dark,
each flash and blur, each crack and sudden fade
of colour an after-image, a faint mark

coming and going in the uncurtained room
where we both sat it out, up in the air,
in the rush and rustle, click and smack and boom
of lights as they sprayed and scattered everywhere.

Least Harm

Enough just to be there,
taken right down, apart
to the frame just, the skeleton,
barely there,
enough to say it enough of that
whatever else again,
but there just, whatever
good it is or it does.

A History Channel

If I watch any more, I'll start to be seen
mostly in black and white, coming and going
in silence, moving too fast, and when I do speak,
speaking continually in a clipped accent;
the friends who recognise me on the screen
where I train binoculars on a white Atlantic
will soon get used to this, to when I'm showing,
and when not to listen to those level, bleak
sentences all about taking it, and going to it,
in an archive voice, brassy with death and the distance.

Stick-figures move a little on the deck
of a corvette sailing placidly away
to join the convoy that will never come back,
and I do what I can to provide a soundtrack
for this or any other last appearance –
You are my sunshine, the pulse of a big band,
and the possibility that skies are grey
is all beyond me, utterly beyond
the vanishing men who vanished long since
in boats and slow freighters into an actual silence.

But it all has to be jaunty and remote
as stagy Greeks, with their archaic manners,
inclining over spears or cigarettes
while they stream forever down the busy channel,
just specks in radar, to flare one by one
in reddened smoke or the cold bitter water;
the shapes you make out are their silhouettes,
black figures walking at you from the sun,
speechless while the programme speaks by rote
in someone's voice: how this is it, and how they go to it.

The Resurrection of the Soldiers

Stanley Spencer

Of course the walls are silent, but
can music be implicit there?
What horns and pumping trumpets, shut
in paint, might blast and shake the air?

What happens when the skies unclose,
and how does the sour ground come fresh?
How freely do the worms compose
their variations on the flesh?

Two Memorials at Gilnahirk

1

He was stuck fast, I suppose, in his twenties,
the soldier who was never to be
my grandfather, who left home for the War
and who died there soon,

obediently, like others, and unremarkably;
who left his wife, and left a pair of sons,
and whose young ghost, as it leaned on the half-door,
watched lives not his fold up and unfold:

my grandmother, with hard years in front of her,
the Dromore man she married, and the hearth cold
when he died, early too; the new children;

his wife then, going blind as she grew old,
more of a stranger to him, with the names of everyone
a muddle; a straight and handsome widow woman.

2

Details that mattered, and still matter, are gone,
and the best I can do with them is pilfer
bits and pieces, for I can't be sure
exactly what it is I'm building on

as I balance and prop and jam together
parts for this rickety memorial:
the soldier's name must have been Moore,
but his Christian name? And my grandfather,

was it Dromara he came from, not Dromore?
I lean invisibly on a boundary wall
to watch over my mother in the next war,

as she reaches to take her brother Sidney's hand
on the Rocky Road, where her brothers Charlie and James,
and even the dog Major, all answer to their names.

Spillage

Night after night, my stare fixed itself on the dark
as if to stare it down – as if – as if to see
form a circle of light would help light break
and leak from the edges into my eyes, insidiously,
like days and days of rain, then pools of rainwater
ready to seep and spill in a wash, a slow flood
of splattery colours that might dry out now, or later,
or never dry in the wet recesses they had filled:

a sky so parched and papery, so low and far
stretched I couldn't see around it, or see past it
(as if wet eyes, sore words or feelings could get past it),
when daylight, broad or rainy, or just dull,
outlasts all this – all that – keeps and dissolves it all
in a standstill: for not a day passes, not an hour.

Words for a Poem

The piece of paper (one piece of paper) these words are written on
  is already in tatters, pulled to pieces and scrunched
up to litter a room – and it's *your* room, in this instance –
  where someone is crying, and someone is silent with rage.
Whatever is up in the air, the air is crackly and bitter,
  unbreatheable, the bits of paper are breaths
ripped away, but they won't go away; at this moment
  tears are all over your eyes, you can't see a stime,
but this page can tell you he's there still, with a face on him
  like a man who has bitten on a clove, or drunk eisel.

The Cloud

Near the beginning, it must be a summer's day,
we are together in a black-and-white garden
in front of the greenhouse, you on your knees
and me with my hands on my knees, our faces level,
and smiling into the sunlight for the camera.
We both look shy there, even of each other,
as we wait to hear the shutter clunk, to get up
and out of the glare, then move further apart
as you go inside to practise the piano
and I am driven home, where I forget all this.

I must be two years old in the photograph
and you are maybe fourteen; can you tell me?
The last time I saw you, I was too shy to speak:
but you are a girl still, and I am a man,
muddled and sour and a grown man
with things to tell you, which you will never hear
as my voice loses its way between us.
Face to face, I touch your cheek with a finger,
and where I breathe now on your smile
a cloud comes. It would take the light from your eyes.

August

I was trying to read, but the terrible lights and splatter
of rain wild on the gutters and tiles, on the back window,
were too much; I touched off the lamp and just watched
houses and trees light up and go dark, then light up again –

nobody out but one couple drenched through, arm in arm,
running; thunder building and collapsing at intervals
like bombs going off across town; and me closed
in the roof, in my crow's nest or eyrie, if that's what it is.

At Rosses Point

The map in my hands is done,
so I walk here in niggling rain
away past the road, its forgotten
corners and slow bends,
its loops and drops and its dead-ends,
until the only thing that's plain
around each curve of the level shore
is somebody – you, then you again –
waiting incredibly for me there.

I might as well be the metal man
who moves not an inch in years
with the sea around him, a lamp in his hands,
as touch your lips or your hair
while your body is vanishing everywhere,
flesh that appears and disappears
in places like this, where light dispels
or conjures it, as the map of my palm
opens and closes on shells, the actual shells.

Travellers

Last night I dreamed he came back from the dead,
wearing the slate-black overcoat I wore
to his Christmas funeral; and what we said
to calm each other shook us all the more,
fragile with love, that old embarrassment,
no secret, or a secret badly kept,
that burst out into pure astonishment
and weeping in the end, for we both wept.

I saw him see me as he saw me last,
with pleasantries and little else to say
(as often, and as usual, in the past),
a formal man, now middle-aged and tall,
in travelling clothes, ready to go away,
when I held and kissed him in the hospital.

The Long Look

On a scooped-out wall, far underground,
after centuries of darkness and no air,
from flaky plaster, just as they were found,
the painted figures flourish and stare
at you, or at no one in particular.

You can't return their looks, or recognise
them always for the strangers that they are:
in fancy dress, and with slow upturned eyes,
all of them seem to be intent elsewhere,
caught up in a distance that is far too far.

But stranger that you are, you see something,
and carry something back up to the light
where vines and flowers, and real birds on the wing
jostle and clutter the edges of your sight
looking sidelong, and different, and not right.

The Road to Rome

Dust in the umbrella pines
that stand and stretch in their gapped lines
on each side of the road sifts in
to colour everything; the din
of snarling Fiats on the stones
below, and the engines' gasps and groans
stop-starting at their different speeds
trouble the sparse grass and the weeds
a little, but they trouble us
more nearly now we leave the bus
and lean as far as we can lean
into the tiny verge between
the headlong cars and a steep ditch,
with noise and heat at such a pitch
that even the road to Hell today

seems safer than the Appian Way.
(At this point, from an antique past,
into my ear in broad Belfast
an unstill voice insists that I
am taking comfort in a lie,
and those two places aren't distinct
but bloodily and always linked.)
I'm otherwise determined though,
for I have to jump, at the word go,
across the cars on their rough ride
and dare myself to the other side,
arriving, as I knew I must,
already caked in sweat and dust.

To come to Rome in August is
an act of some foolhardiness
for those of us unused to heat:
yet here I am, with pounding feet
and a burnt neck, in spite of all
intent on keeping up my crawl
from site to site in morning sun,
then back indoors by the afternoon.
This morning, though it's barely ten,
is one on which more prudent men
would keep to cafés and galleries
and not set out on paths like these
from a roaring road across parched fields
where no tree, however modest, yields
so much as a scrawny shade, until
the track leads up a gentle hill
and issues in an entrance-gate
where guides and other tourists wait
in batches to go underground.

Today I'm to be shown around
by an already priestly youth,
beaming and bursting with the truth,
who comes from India; he leads
a dozen of us, some with beads
to pray by in the better rooms

among the sunken catacombs,
and burbles happily all the while
as he shepherds us, with a sure smile,
down rough steps, over bumpy floors,
into those dull red corridors
that wind and branch and ramify
for miles into the dark, where I
can all too easily begin
to visualise myself, locked in,
a wandering unquiet ghost
lost, and imprisoned with the lost
along the remoter galleries.
For all the snappy homilies
he makes at every turn and twist,
the gloom here helps me to resist
our guide's too zealous overview;
for the sad truths are hardly new:
against death's evidence everywhere
his voice's frail career in air
is something infinitely small,
a single, echoless footfall
where silence takes in everything.
What meagre history I can bring
down with me to these deathly streets
restates, reiterates, repeats
over and over the single rule
taught in its hard and tedious school,
how memory and firm belief
obliged at last to come to grief
perpetuate an old design,
and always need to blur the line
between dumb hope and vanity.
Down passages I scarcely see
the dead ranged once on either side,
but not without some measured pride
in family or faith; they left
tokens behind for the bereft
where rank and virtue could find mention,
as well as for God's best attention,
or for the notice of other gods –

a change of faith made little odds
to the modest or the extravagant
memorials with whose aid they went
out of the buzzing world: one wall
keeps delicate portraits a foot tall,
where, framed by intricate designs
of peacocks, flowers and heavy vines,
intent upon some heavenly crown,
the dear departed stare us down
whose eyes, looking away, look through
us and our own contingent view.

The Indian novice's upbeat
and chatty commentary makes neat
distinctions where things should be blurred:
here, Christ about to give the word
for Lazarus to come, is less
himself than he is Orpheus,
and, working miracles with ease,
shades elsewhere into Hercules.
Despite the martyrs stacked around,
this ground is also pagan ground,
and several tombs on their long lets
seem cannily to be hedging bets
between two worlds at subtle strife
on tickets for the future life.
When some of the better families
moved out from their good premises
in the city, they found here instead
a swish suburbia of the dead
and later, as more Christians came
to swell the ranks, these were the same
addresses that kept up their price
and added features to entice
the faithful here, with martyrs and
late popes in popular demand
(good company for when the skies
roll open, and the bodies rise),
until the district grew at last
a crowded place, with deep and vast

recesses and branching avenues
of the shelved dead in stacks and queues
patiently waiting for the end.
Now, as our chipper Indian friend
lights up the dreary neighbourhood
with the force of his 'the martyrs' blood!',
I'd like to hear the ghosts agree
as they turn in their sleep, and we
leave them secure in stone and clay
to snuggle up till Judgement Day
when Hell and Heaven, black and white,
utter darkness, utter light,
split in an instant, and for ever.

For now, the more mundane endeavour
to keep our footing on the stairs
absorbs us all, as our way bears
narrowly up and sharp around
to the blasting daylight above ground.
As the guide's parting pieties
speed us out on our day-release
I find some shade and, book in hand,
replot the daring route I'd planned
to bring me home, but sense the heat
still rising, and opt to retreat
to *via Appia* and the bus.
Forgetting my gloomy-ponderous
pontifications in the dark,
I'm more than ready to embark
on the road to Rome, and lunch, and soon
siesta through the afternoon.

(At odds with so much here, I want
to air my bumptious, Protestant
certainties and predispositions
– just call them foregone intuitions –
and, fresh from the stale catacomb,
confess myself dyed in the womb
in colours now indelible
I wouldn't want to change at all.

It's ten years on since first I came
to visit Rome, and still the same
gripes and frustrations and ill-will
mingle with every simpler thrill
in plenty here; though deep in thrall
to the peculiar pastoral
(part history and part escape),
I'm haunted often by the shape
of an old enemy on the stones:
the disapproval in my bones
for all the bulging pomp remains
distinct as ever, and maintains
its staunch dissenting line, while I
saunter beneath a Roman sky
and, hammered by the sunshine, lurch
from church to gilded baroque church,
admiring and deploring on
like some off-duty puritan,
delighted and appalled to find
himself so little colourblind.)

The sun high up gets stronger by
the minute, and the minutes fly;
the time for me to set my face
towards a journey home, and pace
myself along the burning track
is more than come; I stagger back,
casting no shadow on the white
path where among the stones a bright
and tiny lizard, green and blue,
has scamper-scuttled into view
for half a second, and is gone
as quickly; pushing on and on,
I trample pale and scalding coals
and come to where the traffic rolls
downhill to Rome; again I make
the leap of faith that is the break-
neck crossing, and I live to see
the further side, and sanctuary:
small houses closed against the heat;

the travellers who stand and wait;
thin fences strung with wire and rust,
and pines the colour of the dust.

An Alarm

At dawn, the gulls call out to one another
and crowd the bedroom with their gawky cries,
so that we waken, as if to a child's cries,
all summer early, with nothing like surprise.

The Blood-Bruise

I worked against it all that afternoon,
the racing bindweed, or convolvulus,
that had gone unchecked, it seemed, by anyone
for weeks, and now made its calamitous
faces everywhere: those deathly-delicate
trompettes, and their lime-white
mouths that opened up, and opened again,
in silent and proliferating forms
strung along cords I had to bundle down
and gather up as tangles in my arms.

I stooped in to the stricken rosebushes
where they had all but given up the ghost
so deeply had the bindweed's ropes and lashes
become involved, and so nearly had they lost
the plot to its inveigling flowers and leaves;
as thorns plucked at my sleeves
I hauled in slippery tendrils by the yard
until my arms could hold no more, my arms
that, now I looked, had been scrabbed and scarred
where they and the sharp roses came to terms.

What I saw then, when I saw you suddenly,
knocked me off-kilter, like a freak shot
or a punch from nowhere, making light of me:
it wasn't even your face at first, and not
your blue-green eyes as they took in my alarm,
but the blood-bruise on your arm
where the skin was softest; where, as I looked,
I almost tracked the course a vein might run
minutely under my fingers; where they unhooked
and undid you, when all of their work was done.

Standstill

There is a house where all the doors are closed:
I can see this house from the outside in,
and they watch me, looking from the inside out
at a morning, a particular one in the autumn,
with somebody there just standing under the trees
who can look in and see them still looking
back at him, wondering when he will come,
as he asks himself why he left, and when he did,
why each step forwards is a step further away
from a house with all the windows and the doors closed.

A Fall

I wake up from a dream about being in America
to a blackbird holding its own against the early traffic;
in the dream, I was jumping on solid ground
to prove that it was there, as the blackbird also proves itself
in a bleary dawn, where now fog proves that it is autumn.

The Conversion

Then in September came the plague of spiders.
How many tens or dozens
in the one week might have slipped inside
and set up shop with threads and muslins
strung out from the corners, I could hardly tell;
but they found me everywhere, at all hours,
as they raced down walls, or hared along the floors,
tumbling, or sticking at a point, deathly still.

So the spiders took possession of my house
and I, convinced they were unlucky to kill,
left them to their businesses in autumn rooms
and closed the doors
to settle, touchily, in a dark place
and coddle in my hands a pint of gall.

The Risk

The chances are this won't work:
taking in swatches of early light
(half-light, either early or late)
these sore eyes tell me I'm awake

and now, whatever the chances are,
the game and I no longer match,
for I can't win, or win much,
with losses harder and harder to bear –

downturns, upsets, all-out collapse,
a dead-end at the end of luck
where I might stick, or might be stuck,
waiting for sudden breaks and slips

in the brilliant game being played through
before my eyes, its risk of loss
as nothing to this need to lose
it all now on one losing throw.

The Mild Autumn

I'm back, and the mild autumn is here too,
where by this time in October usually
the trees are stripped down, and a flooding wind
has come with sleet and cold, to stay for good.

But this year we are having a mild autumn,
and I am home to see you in October
when every day the sun keeps flooding
into these rooms where, for a while, I'll stay

and where, for a while, we have each other back,
so that today I needn't watch my time
as we wait, not saying much, and half shut down,
for the pools results or the next meal to come.

With the winter holding back for good, we both
suppose that this might usually be the way,
that the winds will keep down, and the cold
evenings and days will not come, after all;

suppose I may stay here, or might never have gone,
where the trees with all their leaves in flood
are never stripped, and where the night comes down
without a breath of cold when it comes to stay.

Two Spiders

The first has been dead for a long time
– and this is, in any case, a long time ago –
when it falls, or it drops, or slow-slides
out of a book I've opened and won't read
(in the bedroom, in the sunlight, in an odd moment)
next to weightless in my palm.
This is a black spider, and the book
has a dedication in copperplate French
where the dark ink has faded and blurred slightly,
to whom, and from whom, I don't know.

The other spider suddenly came to light
as I leaned and caught a sleeve in the hedge,
and it fiddles with my shirt-cuff for dear life now
over a precipice, till I cup it in a palm
where it is waiting, or I make it wait,
for one thing or the other. It's a blurry white
against the colour I am, or my hand is,
like a letter fading out or fading in from somewhere
that might belong to any standard message
sent from the dead to the dead, for no reason.

Hush

Speak these words, in this order, pause
where rest is called for; it will not be my voice
you hear, or sound like mine: there is no choice
but to accept this, and no other cause
to plead against pure silence at the end
except to say (and softly, slowly say)
that nothing will replace the sounds today
the hedges make here, as they give and bend
with the invisible mild breeze
that comes from nowhere, simmering and seething
up through acres of fields and miles of trees

until it reaches this blind place, like grief,
like one long sob without change or relief;
but it's not that. When I breathe, it's not me breathing.

Leopardi

Seashells

As I look now, you are starting to look through me,
out as far as wherever the tide has gone,
while clouds bundle sunlight from Inishowen
over our heads, and our slow walk, rained-on,
into a windy glare of salt and ozone
is something very gradually lost to view.

These empty shells are brittle as your bones,
and here's one with a thread of amber-brown
that runs around then runs out in a spiral
into my palm. Now I am the colour of sand
on soft ground paved with only shells
for your hazel eyes, that are starting to cloud over.

The Full House

For decades, when you think of Union Street,
you mention how one night the house was crammed
so tightly men lay on the stairs and landing,
– travellers in this and that, from all parts –
one slumped half-upright by a corner wall,
one wedged under a table; and all but you
are sleeping there, packed in and packed away:
motionless all the night, they never waken.

Work: 1998

These buildings are heartbroken for the city –
it failed them, and they failed it, long ago;
even dignity has been saved too long here,
and it turns bad in a faint tide of spring air
where I must walk more than a mile uphill,
past the same places to work every day:
the places hurt me now; maybe we hurt each other.

Time wastes the stone. Some quarrels are past mending:
the word is attrition, a sure wearing-down,
pointless and relentless like the weather;
meetings are a circus of self-regard,
a freakshow, where the dwarf and the lion-lady
are trapped in themselves, and stuck with each other
for good, and where I too am a fixture.

Everyone fails: my heart works overtime,
pumping round venom and gall; it wears down
all concerned, till the rooms stink of exhaustion.
Time drains into the stone, and drains away
like the sweat of slaves, while I learn the tricks
and turns of a performer, trained to do
business with the implacable and the mad.

At night, I half-run downhill to the station,
past places that can tear me up in ribbons
and mean to; my heart stalls and starts again,
and it all goes through me like a lifting wave,
transparent, if not clear; treading a void,
I watch my steps leading me everywhere
on a fast road, deliberate and faithless.

The Stand-Off

To say anything now is to risk it all:
and both of them know how it is all risk
at this proximity; how it's somebody's call,
as they stare each other out like basilisk
and gorgon; how it's someone's turn to break
rank, even a rank of one, for form's sake.

Perhaps they were lovers once, or may become so –
it doesn't matter: what they say in the end
will be formal and inscrutable, for show,
full of what has been and what might be said,
and in no language that can give or bend.

Ready to take each other to their knees,
they stand on motionless by the made bed
with faces set, guests of the thief Procrustes.

The Thread

How slightly, twenty years ago,
I managed to construe the girl
I met three times, or twice, then so
awkwardly flirted with, by proxy,
dispatching printed poems of mine
whose frail and thin-spun lines
took scarcely any weight (I see
that much), carried no weight at all.

In a bored moment, by sheer chance,
news of her death crosses my eyes,
and minutes pass while I realise
that now, at this far distance,
I can't so much as picture her,
feeling for the least snag or pull
in a line that's barely visible,
and slighter than a thread of hair.

Damon the Mower

The beer in my fist is a bar of gold, and bitter;
the taste in my mouth is only the taste of cold.
I watch the punters, and see people who aren't here,
catching in a girl's drunk laugh another's shriek-sob
as she tells and blurts and gasps out what has to be told:

how some yob in a suit thinks he thinks the whole world of her;
how he dresses her up in shoes and stockings and lace and gold;
how he loves her so much, he took the blunt stub of a glass and
hit her;
how I'm her last and only hope, her one true friend:
how it's come to an end, though it's always coming to an end.

I'm tasting again the salt-bitter tears on her cheek
as I drink down shots of alum, vinegar, eisel, gall,
to take the first and only dope, this mild and meek
fall-guy down for a fall, a taste of blood and bruises,
like a man who asks *What is it?* and knows rightly what it is.

The Way to Lose

Tonight again I thought I could see your face crying,
but in a mirror, and only reversed, dry tears
coated my cheeks and my lips, as I watched the lying
words come out backwards: this for months; for years.

Fireworks

in memory of Sheila Smyth

1

As I walked to the appointment with you at my heels,
I could hear my own steps fall on the pavement
and was thankful for the gravity of new shoes
with their sounding weight against the clean-washed stone.
I thought I might be leaving a trail of sparks,
but knew if I looked round there would be only
daylight, no glimmer-glitz, and no glamour
of faceted and soon-gone lightning; no,
not you even, whom I'd just asked along
to lend what weight you could to the proceedings,
and keep up with me for these last few paces.

2

It was like putting a match
to a tablet, or a lozenge,
then starting to watch
this dot with a fizz and fringe
of tiny sparks flare up
in the blacked-out sitting-room:
above the saucer a beam,
a pillar of deep light
that would rasp, change colour, then drop,
at its prime some five or six
inches tall, if that.

We had bought indoor fireworks:
in half an hour, an entire box
had been set up, set off,
and burned away (no match
for the real thing, and no
real thing that year anyhow).

They didn't come to much,
but I said I liked them, half
to please people, half
to reassure myself; and now,
in daylight, look: a room
where the dead sit down with strangers
after tea at Hallowe'en;
laid out in the middle of this
are fireworks like sweeties –
jelly beans, pastilles, and cinnamon
lozenges (properly, *lozengers*).

3

I was going somewhere fast, or seemed to be:
I remember the hurry, the blind panics and flare-ups,
me lying awake all night in Dunluce Avenue
hearing everything in the world that ever moved;
but up in the air mostly, with the illusion of speed,
and the conviction that I must be weightless.
While the ground beneath me seemed to vanish,
you knew what to say and what not to say.

I did nothing – stuck, weighed down, engrossed even –
after our friend had told me you were dying:
the right or the wrong words wouldn't have mattered,
and what I took for speed was just things moving
in one direction all the time, with me
slow to make ground: too slow, if anything.

Eclogue

It's as though the fields around these parts
had been written over as well as worked
for generations: cuneiform straws
tumble and stick across the ground
for me and a few sorry birds
to worry over, as the day ends
in bluster and half-hearted rain.
A car drips quietly in the lay-by,
unlocked, and with the engine warm,
as I get ready to return,
picking a way through the ditch-side
scatter of votive offerings –
bottles, chip-papers, crunched-up cans
of *Harp* lager – and I keep one eye
on the familiar glare and steam-boil
of clouds and sun on this horizon
changing the weather over and over.
This time tomorrow, I'll be gone
– or back to where I'm gone from now –
and the light and drizzle, the baffling wind,
that come and go on the Castlereagh hills
all morning and all afternoon
will come and go again, without me.

Come on – for you know rightly now
it's time for you to be away:
in an hour or two, the shuttle flight
will put your head back in the clouds,
heaving you up over the shipyard
and out across the water again.
In your mind's eye, you see this place
from the air mostly, reduced to shapes,
clouds and cloud-shadows, farms, towns,
always becoming smaller and more
blurred in the melancholy distance.
Down here, things sharpen and mean less:
it's not the best place, not the worst.

I envy you the grip and focus
on everything I can't possess:
I'm lost to home, as home is lost

to me, and there's no going back –
just visiting and visiting,
where my mind puts a shadow down
across the landscape, drained away
into near-perpetual dusk.

What happens here is real, mundane:
dusk only comes at daylight-fall,
and lives get led without you here.
You look at the high Braniel road
and see it thirty years ago:
I wasn't born then, and the whole
bad-time history leaves me cold.
You're hypnotised by the stupid past,
and just because you can't get loose
from its clutches, you expect to preen
your feathers while you lick your wounds,
then turn the lot into dismay
and sadness that seeps everywhere
in the end, doomy, absolute.
If you knew it, there's a future too –
not glamorous, maybe, but it's there;
and every detail of the day
can scarcely answer to the gloom
you always want to paint across it:
there's money here, and the normal mix
of family, routine, good times;
no need for me to shrink or cringe,
for I'm secure with what I am
and don't need to apologise.
Isn't that better? And the truth is
there's peace now – peace: you can hardly
bring yourself to say the word.

I'm never at peace, for it's one thing
or another that distresses me,
distracts me, through the day and half
the night; but most of all, simply
these hills and roads, the people here,
or here no longer, the thin ghosts:

I keep on looking out for them
or listening for their voices in mine.
One summer night, on the walk up
from the Knock Road to Mann's Corner,
Charlie Moore saw the crooked back
and shoulders, and the bowed-down head
of an old farmer, sitting still
on a wall, who had worked the land
a century before; the Rocky Road
at Gilnahirk, still overgrown
when I was young, a boundary
between our steps and the graveyard,
keeps watch over the newly dead
and my own father now, a guest there.
To see peace, and peace only, is
to see the living and not the rest,
as though to shade your eyes in sun
and pick your way through grassy ruins,
scarcely able to look up.
That's why the light and shadows here
transfix me, why some future is
an abstract blur against the sharp
presence of figures in this landscape.
Nothing is new, and it can't be:
liars who talk about history
as something whose warm hand they feel
guiding them in a chosen path
vanish, and never answer to
all of the anger or the grief;
their words hide most of what they mean,
and when they smile into your face,
they don't mean words. It's time to go.
From here, the lights of Belfast look
like a huge diagram, with the city
a puzzle putting itself together
by trial and error, piece by piece,
as traffic bellows into the sky.

We'll go together on the drive,
and maybe have the time for one

more coffee in Departures; look,
the last of the sun is cutting straight
through the hedgerow, and our two
thin shadows have begun to stretch
into each other along the road.

The Company

They're not all old, and he's about my age,
this one who waddles out of his road towards me
and says what he can; I say back what I can,
then hear him breathing his way on to somewhere.

The bald man with no bowels left is searching
for his absent brother, and looks even under the beds
about this time every night; he keeps asking
the same question, and not hearing the same replies,

while a boy with plummy eyes and a mashed face
takes ten minutes to get out of his bed,
to assemble himself, his legs and his purple arms
with minutest care, and wait outside then for nothing.

Everybody gets what's coming: even the police
know this, who can set questions about bones
and bruises unknown to the doctors; missing persons
keep company with visitors in their cars

all the way home, and they stay not there
like a pain that's gone and might be coming back
when some little something
grows, and takes hold, and finds out what it's looking for.

The Proof

One birthday I came to see you out of the blue,
and walked in on you, in your usual chair,
and a flood of papers, pools-coupons and pens,
where, just for a second, you looked me through
and through, as though between us a cloudy lens
gave grounds for doubt that I was there at all.
The proof is there if you want it to be there:
once I had left my bag down in the hall
I came on in, and came back in to normal.

Our manners held, and still they hold us steady,
for although I don't appear now just for form's sake,
I seem to know the proper way to find you,
busy as ever, waiting there at home,
as if we knew the best way to make ready,
the two of us, by instinct, and by proof:
silently almost, and while I've hardly noticed,
you have made your way out of the sitting-room,
closing the door very quietly behind you.

The Back Roads

You had come so close, that when I woke
to the phone, and answered half-asleep,
there was a voice from the dead that spoke
to a sunken distance – faint, miles deep –

at a loss to figure some way back
and calling from the further bank
to the son who lost you – who lost track
of plastic boats that dipped and sank,

or a kite that crashed at the Giant's Ring,
the loop-the-loops and vanishing-tricks
of gliders, tangled yards of string,
then crumpled balsa and splintered sticks

all lost, and your voice with them lost –
but I came to, and the voice was real,
no rivers and no lines were crossed,
no boat with a crimped and crinkled sail

or aeroplane with bent-back wings
had come to grief in the water there;
as usual, we said usual things
on our back roads to everywhere.

The Watercolourists

It is six in the evening in the nineteenth century,
and I join the watercolourists on the Aventine
who are all sitting forwards in one straggly line
completely intent, and never noticing me,
as they work and watch, quickly, silently,
to catch the sky in a violet bruise or a stain
that seeps into their paper, almost weighing it down,
the distant and near colours all that they can see.

Rome is below us, where sheep still haunt the Forum,
and I know I am with the busy dead, for here
is my own great-grandfather, John Graham,
who studies the view, and paints one field in Ayrshire
for ever, utterly engrossed; in a flutter and flare
of light and water, I start work with the least of them.

THE HOUSE OF CLAY

2007

San Domenico

My road from the bus-stop
takes me up twenty feet of steps
between high concrete walls
infested with scrubby dust and wasps,
graffiti, litter-falls,
and everywhere, from feet- to head-height,
gouged and scored, cut left and right
with bullet-holes

from fifty years ago
worn-in and weathered, that will stay so
for another fifty years,
where lizards scoot and insects go
forth, and back and forth
from shade to sun, while no one sees,
busy all afternoon for centuries
in the hot earth,

as I walk a few yards
down a line of stunned or basking cars
and the silent hospital,
then gates, and their stone eagle-guards
that look straight down the hill
as they take the longest of all long views
on walking men, just small enough to lose,
who hug the wall

as shelter from the sun
that burns straight down without reason
in the day's dead part,
and go home for the afternoon
to wait in shuttered light
half-reading books already half-read
with fruit and water and dry bread
and no appetite –

my destination too,
where I wait it out, as I have to,
with papers and ornaments
I can look over and look through,
a pile of cards unsent,
maps, glasses, and a handful of leaves
I cut this morning from three graves,
a kind of present

to myself, part souvenir
and part *memento mori*, laid out where
they wait to age and dry;
in the few hours till I appear
again on this last day
I open and close old books of lives,
smoothing their pages, to fill the first leaves
with leaves of bay.

The Hand

1

A flat right hand: four fingers and a thumb,
and poised, as though to strike an instrument,
fend off a blow, or maybe stop the waves.

Each evening, it would blatter on the glass
of our front window like a thunderclap,
not breaking it, stretching our nerves past breaking.

2

Thirty years on, and I can't not drive
in this direction, just to see the place.
There's nothing much here, nobody about:

Stormont up in the hills, unearthly white
as ever, new houses eating up the fields;
but I forget more now than I remember.

Leaving, I see the parti-coloured kerbstones
with paint from last year or the year before
that fades into this almost-constant rain,

then, on one gable-wall, a raised right hand.

3

It took a full two minutes to run down
from the bus terminus to our front door:
in the last year, I skipped and swerved and darted

all the way back, with tiny ricochets
of stones at my legs and heels. All spring
I ran, and ran so fast I couldn't stop.

4

We lived in 44A Woodview Drive,
across the road, and just a few doors down
from an apprentice murderer, who learned

his trade in town, and then came home for tea.
The hard skin in my palm is like soft stone:
as I look at it now under the desk-light,

calloused and scuffed and bitten and worn-in,
this part of me is guiltless flesh and bone,
whatever it has done or might yet do.

5

Leaving means going away for the last time,
unnoticed now, hardly worth noticing:
up in the distance, Stormont, unearthly white.

I forget more than I remember – how
this road connects to that, the way to town,
the names of people who lived there, or there.

As I move faster, everything speeds up:
I make the rain stop by raising my hand,
and sunlight loses itself on the Castlereagh hills.

As Seen

The house of stone,
too visible
in its one field,
dumb as a sign
you see for miles,

without a purpose
or a purpose long
gone, not known,
is always now
no home to us

now home is gone,
like the last field
of stone and clover,
and there's no sign
of us, or for us,

in that place, where
the visible ground
rises for miles,
then without purpose
it goes down

beneath the horizon
to pitch and turn
with an invisible
cargo of bodies
that pitch and turn

and that run rings
around the sky
till dusk or dawn
(no more than in
the way of things),

so no one sees
except ourselves
the dark and plain
lights in a mesh
of wires for miles

and in desperation
we force ourselves
to our bare flesh
again, and again
in desperation

as a dumb sign,
but miles away;
the tangled cry
not ours, not known;
the house of clay.

Cetacea

1

There and then, he takes a big breath

and pelts across the wooden floor
which is also the Atlantic Ocean,
to surface in front of everyone
dumbfounded on the near shore,
hoisting water by the ton
as a weightless, fast Leviathan
who cuts through elements, and sails
along with the sea-shouldering whales.

2

Late summer air: not a breath.
Across town the invasion bells
are silent, as heat coats the hills
to make them wave and tremble; hares
and birds lie low in fields of corn
while the one sound that he hears
is his own voice with the same phrase
falling in wild woods forlorn:
a little dead march that replays
its slow, unshoulderable weight,
portending sickness in the state.
Forlorn. The very sound of that.

3

Sea creatures out of their element
must know about the air's weight
beneath which lungs are bent
and twisted into knots and cramps,
while all they can do is wait,

caught in some remote *impasse*
between breath and the body: this
carries with the sounding surf
into the snort and water-puff
of a beached, exhausted grampus
not able to breathe.

Clearout

So much to be got rid of, that will go
anyhow in the end – *that* doleful saw –
stares me in the face: an *imbroglio*
of hosepipes, wire mesh, and a rusted saw
with broken flowerpots and old tools below
in this particular shed, on this one day,
all mine to sort out or to throw away.

Relentless summer rain softens the wood
as I take shelter in a box of dust
and breakage, junk and waste and solitude.
Fears in solitude. The sleep of the unjust.

★

Today, my fortieth year begins to end,
and either I am taking up more space
or else the walls really do start to close
on me, and leave me barely room to stand
up straight under the rain-beat, the rain-purr;
more lost, more stuck; duller and drowsier.

★

I waken with my arms crossed on my chest
as if I were lying on a bed of stone,
in a vaulted room that points towards the east,
around me a dozen keepsakes and talismans
to see me through, however long the wait:

dolls with the heads of animals, one flat
and stranded figurine, the shadow-puppet,
pieces of brick and bubbles of clear glass,
old schoolbooks maybe, photographs.
                                        These things
aren't mine, and this must be three years ago,
surrounded by some other man's belongings,
but not here – stopped in Italy for two
bad-tempered, haunted weeks, and sheltering
in the tiny chamber every afternoon,
stopped dead, pretending to be pressing on.

⋆

The rain stop-starts. Wood squeaks and clicks.
I bring out bin-bags and a list of tasks.

The Gnat

So up he got, moving numb legs and arms
that didn't want to move, he was so tired.
Breath was one sigh recurring; in one sigh
the grief rose in his chest, and then it broke
like a wave, collapsing everywhere at once –
grief, that is, for the gnat
                              whose ghost had spoken
all night on the subject of death, last things,
that other world beneath the world we know
where the antique and celebrated shades,
as dead as one another, do their time
in gloomy dungeons or in strange, pale fields;
the gnat, whose well-meant bite had woken him
just as a snake, with trouble on its mind,
came sliding up from nowhere to his side;
the gnat whom, without thinking, he had swiped
into perdition with one ignorant hand –
grief for the poor gnat swelled inside, almost
to bursting, as he went about his task.

First he cleared out the brambles and the weeds
that clumped together above a trickle-down
stream of pure rainwater; he took a spade
and dug out a circle, till a round of earth
stood as a simple rampart for the tomb.
This he patched up with mosses; then he searched
out the best stones from the stony hillsides,
pink- and white-veined marble, a full dozen,
and set them up together in a ring
slowly, with minute care; next, he assembled
bulbs and slips to plant for a grave-garden –

acanthus, with roses all red and purple,
a scatter of every kind of violet
to grow among the hyacinths and rare
crocuses, below a single laurel tree;
juniper then, with marigolds, and a trail
of ivy glittering in the sun like steel;
a flowering vine, narcissi underneath,
rosemary, and the bitter herb called Patience.

Last, on a plaque, in his own silent letters,
he spelled out terms of penitence and sorrow:
the debt owed to a solitary gnat,
and this repayment, too late in the day.

from *Culex* (*Appendix Virgiliana*)

Literal

Why should it be the flesh,
its muscle stretched or plush,
and the vulnerable skin
alert or dead to touch,
holding the body in
where blood and bones attach

that rises, if it does,
unwanted or desired,
the pulsebeat as it was
in a pitted body scarred
deep with its own likeness;
why should the flesh come back

to sense, and the senses' weight
return, and the skin's lightness,
unless this body's rack
of bones and intricate
fine sinews, so degloved,
marked out the literal

truth, even in disrepair;
its sadness or tired fall
as strength and force remove;
the five senses eternal,
busy again with love's
design or love's despair?

War Diary

The light of the new moon and every star
concentrates now in a reflection
of trailing grasses and cow-parsley
from a puddle; clear glass is a mirror
as the night goes up into action
on wet roads, never to return:
the country roads long since taken,
known mile by mile, yard by yard,
and still abandoned. What did I see there?
Who, maybe? Some such question.

The Moth

Half-daylight, and the summer stars
come out from far back in the sky
in ones and twos, still hard to see
while a temperate, short night prepares
itself to fall, but gradually,
across and into everything
light edges now, or shines along.

From somewhere in the lilac bush,
a moth has come before its time:
it blunders between purple bloom
and shadow, with the palest brush
of its wings, grainy white and dim,
then vanishes, or moves away
from where our glances barely stay.

I imagined that I saw the wings,
throughother, tattered, broken past
mending, between shadows cast
here and there, or the scattering
japs of light where branches pressed
into each other along the shade
that flowers and our own bodies made.

Too early, and hard to notice then,
pale things get lost against the light.
The garden and its trees soon let
their shadows fatten, like those thin
designs that didn't come out right,
but waited for their time to grow –
surviving now, for all we know.

The Other World

after Pindar

Wild grasses, bleached, miles of them;
no sun in the glaring sky:

it is night time, so this must be
somewhere beneath the earth.

In all-over light, for ever, the grass makes
stars and rivers and waves of the sea.

Strongman

1

Bowed down, bowed under,
in his two hands, what?
A book? Or some creature
he wants to escape
more than he wants to keep?

With eyes and palms unshut,
knees bending where the steep
path started to scrape them,
he looks in wonder
at the weightless place

2

at the weightless place
between his hands
where wings maybe clapped
this minute
and the air went out of place
while it just leapt

away, while it took flight,
whatever it was,
to fast clouds and headlands
far up from where he looks
at his hands, at a pivot,
at an empty space

3

so light air fails
and no release
comes for the eyes;
no turning away
from these things
glazed and dead

that move, that ease
themselves to heads and
limbs of men
with their skins that turn
now to feathers, scales,
and the faces of beasts.

Spoils

Our taxi sails on an open road
where they have paved the wilderness –
unending hilly scrub-land

that later I look out across,
as night falls, from the balcony
of a house in a new town,

spotting arc-lights between the sky
and the next hill, watched in my turn,
while masts of concrete and steel

frame building-sites against the moon,
darken themselves, and then grow tall,
taking their certain bearings from

a fenced road to Jerusalem:
late, and better late than soon.

The Overcoat

We stop, and doors come open then
to let the early dark blow in
from whatever rain-raked platform
is just outside the lighted train,
as men who lined up in a storm
crush in to seats, bringing a chilled
February air along with them,
agents for winter afternoons
and *entrepreneurs* of the cold.

On business now, and going home,
I'm no more than a few steps from
Belfast in 1972:
the cigarette smell is the same
in the same draught, that pushes through
with men who walk in envelopes
of smoke and cold from a slow queue
and onto buses with no room
in the stops and starts, the hold-ups.

Behind me by a couple of hours,
in winter downpours, sleet-showers,
he comes by bus from Inglis's,
and the breadmen and the bakers,
to town, and waits again, and catches
the number 24 or 32
home, back over his own traces,
to a breezeblock, ground-floor
Braniel flat; to damp and mildew.

Where he hangs up his overcoat
the cold begins to radiate,
shaped out, like the body's ghost,
by the hall door at night;
and now the cold that presses past
me here is maybe a ghost's trail,
the time it fills already lost
and its place lost in an infinite
line of shapes: indistinct, frail.

On Friday nights, the coat sealed up
some toy bought from a closing shop
for a shilling or for one and six,
coming to me still cold, its shape
and size all cold, a cardboard box
with a soldier or a car inside,
and the toy and winter night would mix
together, as outside would slip
inside: with gifts, and little said.

He was late one night, and came in
quietly; quietly sat down
and ate his tea, then told us how
at work for half the afternoon
the bakery had hosted two
men with guns, their faces masked,
who lined them all up in one row
on the cold floor, to wait, locked in,
for pointed questions to be asked.

The two men left eventually.
Whoever they had come to see
that day they missed, and would find
easily on some other day;
so, standing where they had been lined
up, as if in some anteroom,
everyone talked as they stayed behind,
smoking, and wondering, and free.
Little to do then but go home.

Beside me, a grey overcoat
in the train here is sending out
a smoky aura of sheer cold
invisibly in the carriage-light;
but when I get up, and take hold
of a case packed with dead papers
and a book or two, I come home late,
weighed down with chilly racing cars
and with brittle plastic soldiers.

A Schoolboy

The struggle of the fly
in marmalade might have been
less hopelessly in vain

than the hopeless struggle
to right itself and fly
of my captive bluebottle

held down by the blade
of a modelling knife:
all the signs of life

were showing, to no end,
while I pressed it for blood
with a heavy hand,

and it leaked eggs and ichor
in the romper-room,
the torture-floor

where I was at home –
the legs, the tiny head
working, working away

to the very last,
when it was beheaded
by the wicked schoolboy

in whose direction I cast
this baleful stare,
a theatrical glower,

as if that could pretend
a love of the world,
of true things, not fiction,

the given, not the willed;
as if to order guilt, and
serve it in action.

Windows

1

The square shop window (not really
a shop – a single retail-unit
let by the quarter) has been given
a once-over with a wet cloth
and thin whitewash, so that circles
loop on each other and overlap
in pale and dirty greys, the swirls
making no pattern: somebody
wrote backwards with his finger from
the inside, in not quite English,
LAST DAYS ALL MUST GO,
before he closed the door on it all
and took away what hadn't gone
some night when the last shop had shut.

2

The window-lights in Queen's Arcade
were starting to go out, as I
pressed my nose and fingers hard
up against the cold plate glass

of a sweetshop, where biscuit bears
in cartoon icing seemed to prance
and wave at me from the inside;
for minutes then I screamed and wept
to have those bears from the closed shop,
while the glass bloomed with breath and tears
around my handprints, and outside
the streets were starting to light up
on a Saturday night, drizzle-glazed
for headlamps where they came and went.

Three Rivers

for Louisa

Isis

When you were born, the night sky broke to let fall
its rainwater for hours, and then for days,
then for a week at last, a week of rain,
so that I drove you home over a causeway
with fields submerged on either side of us
where the river spilled across and kept spilling,
the same river that twenty years before
I walked beside on a late October morning,
homesick, crash-landed, watching the slick water
and hearing over and over the words, *How like,*
How like, How like an angel came I down,
straining my eyes in case they broke with tears;
the river that seemed once to swell in sunlight
when it ran like an illuminated margin
beside me later, and the step-by-step
inevitable love, which started here
and brought us here, held safe and moving fast
on a road over acres of floodwater,
sending us home through rain and daylight fall.

Lagan

Down, step by step, and along the bumpy path
he used to follow here, day in, day out,
I took by the arm at last, slow and unsteady
in the blank sunlight of the seventieth spring
since he had lived here in a river cottage
now gone for ever, like that spring itself,
your grandfather, who leaned on me, and looked
through me towards the place at another time –
his run and walk and run all the way to town
along the river, or the soldiers training
across that field, who had to run until
their feet bled; or some other time entirely,
when it is you who take me by the arm
to bring me slowly past Shaw's Bridge, and past
Minnowburn, to the spot where the cottage was,
an old man who moves gently and with pain
talking to you in silences and sounds:
as afternoon lets in the sound of the river,
you help him down the worn and bumpy towpath.

Jordan

We saw the big grey fish deep in the river
as shadows and reflections from above
where we sat on the bankside steps at last,
letting the water slip into our hands
and watching colours come to near the surface
of creatures so small they were hardly fish
but green and gold half-lights, dissolved there
glittering at angles in the straight-down sun
– *How bright, How bright* – that searched the shallow bed
until the sky was shining underneath us;
the quickened surface and deep calm below
were imaged in each other, we in them,
two bodies made of frail and heavy earth,
one bending up to scoop the busy water
into a bottle held firm in the light –

your mother, who moves with you, step by step,
across the sky from one bank to the other
on a well-worn, inevitable path
that goes waist-high and waist-deep in the river.

The Pattern

1

A door too low to be a door:
on the threshold
                    a stepped slab
he stands first where I'm standing
not first not last
                    and then inside –

or so he must have stood.

2

One step another step
                              or every other
repeats itself along the dark,
the slip and pock and blip
of a line on black
screens, arched over like
a tunnel
                    this tunnel
where every step
                    the first the last
is every other step.

3

Crusader vaults, basalt-black,
and a flight of stairs carved down,
a sweep
cut block by block
takes me beneath the ground
takes him with me
already here, far under
the twisting olive trees
that clutch thin soil and dust
behind, above us both
barrelled together in the rock.

4

This is the very door
– no door, a gate
with light far behind –
and the very place
the place here
to stand and wait
in the dark and heat
together here.

5

He scarcely watches me
a child
who stares into the fire
where coals burn down
to crumbly ash in the grate,
and drop into heaps of ash.

6

No door ajar
and no one here
but me, my every step
already to be taken
taken already,
knee-deep
in ashes that fall from bars
above my head,
– fall like snow-smuts
from the bars of the grate
neither cold nor hot –
my head laid bare.

Syrian

Beside a road that belts through the desert,
are a scatter of children, three or four dogs,
and, further back, a few goats, or sheep,
with the women out of sight
inside those far-off, conical houses
made out of clay, the shape of beehives:
and that's more or less everything.

The thousand-km turning to Baghdad
has been and gone, but now, all day,
a straight road goes straight on to Palmyra:
vacant remains chiselled into the sunset
and the oasis-line of palms, a palm-tree
wall blocking out Tadmor, and that
prison nobody knows or talks about.

I will rise with the sun, and walk
for half an hour across cleared ground
into ruins cluttered at the desert's edge,
hiding there among cold
stones as they start to heat up for the day

(not hidden, though, and in that
respect at least unlike too many)

while clay houses and stone houses collude
with silence and bare daylight: that combination.

The Fob-Watch

If I searched, my search for it was brief:
a minute or two in cupboard-boxes,
quick, like a vandal or a thief,
and there it was, the silver still
untarnished, and its rounded, milled
winder over an axle, or an axis
on which this circle turned and turned,
decades ago, in my own hand.

I must have brought the watch with me
en route for Dundonald hospital,
wanting its shape, solidity,
and heaviness all close to hand –
a face I could just understand
for what it was, learning to tell
the time, and watching little else:
the seconds, and their even pulse;

the minute-hand with its thin point
which, staring hard, I could see move
across the dial; and the faint
hint, the faint hope, proffered in one
short arm, that might be moving on
as I was looking, hard to prove,
while I searched the ivory face, to show
the time left, or time still to go.

Transfixed in bed, I hardly spoke
to visitors, or glanced at them;
I was the boy whose patient look

rested beyond all apprehension
on the fob-watch with a pure devotion
to cased and ornamented time
diminishing before my eyes:
a known and true and solid size,

weighed up again now in my palm,
as the closed shape is closing in
on all the tiny, packed and calm
world of a stopped mechanism,
where the dark backward and abysm
recede untouchably, all gone
from substance, weight; from everything:
time is time left, diminishing.

Against the Fear of Death

As the car boils
with sunshine, stuck,

and my hand feels
around the slippery

pudge and stubble
of my own chin,

in the heat again
that sweetsour smell,

your forehead chill
to the touch with sweat,

our two heads then,
our two faces

(ages past, the same
as now, or just then),

mine against
your frightened face

like the white pages
at the end of a book,

between gasps of pain
as we just waited,

and out there, behind
the slatted blind

that put light in threads
across your eyes,

a bright-blotted sky
too white to look at.

Mar Sarkis

I sampled the priest's home-brew
and his tapes of the Lord's Prayer
recited in strong Aramaic
(the original, for all I knew)
before trying out the stairs
cut in rock, and the tiny door

so low that I had to stoop
into candle- and mosaic-
light, then stop
for twenty minutes, half an hour,
in front of Bacchus and Sergius;
there on the stone floor,

watched by those two imperious
big-eyed, mounted soldiers
whose haloes had worn through,
I said words like a foreigner:
I bent double in grief
and prayed for your life.

In Heaven

The distance starts to glow,
half-solid now,

and shapes step slowly
out, one by one

from the horizon,
then they soften

into drumlins, row
upon neat row

of saplings, head-
high, barely moving,

and we walk side by side,
as if our hands touched,

through the small fields;
through the small fields

side by side.

*

Neither farm- nor townland
nor unapproved road;

neither fields of the dead
nor the holy ground

once more, for the light
is not the same:

the horizon round
blushes, and even the air

is larger, so we wear
clothes made of the light,

and the sun
we see by is our own;

and the many stars
when they start to shine.

The Anniversary

A whole year since.
My first-thing glance
of winter today:
our stretch of grass
gone pewter-grey,
with the trees exposed
and brittle with cold;
one silent road
white as a graze.

Close up, my breath
thickens the glass;
it blooms and smears,
then fades as fast
as it came: and there
are the slippery path,
some yards of bare
hard soil, and the cars
blinded with frost.

Inventory

White walls and ceilings; a pallor of wood;
light from no quarter, as broad as it's wide;

daylight – not daylight, but everything else;
two shapes on the bed, one true and one false;

the quiet of clock-time repeating itself
on steel-clear mirrors on no one's behalf

but for everyone's good, while the work goes on
with nobody here, or you here alone

to take down the names from a brilliant wall,
to polish and burnish, and not bewail

the uncountable dead, with their elegies spun
thinly to nothing, and bleached to oblivion,

though not on your time. Categories shift
where the strips of beech-wood are whited and stiff,

and light at no angle gives no quarter
to glasses or blinds or shadows on plaster

as letters come round in backwards reflection,
jumbled, untouchable, sometimes uncertain,

with particulars glaring: the fall of a sparrow;
the bringing together of technique and sorrow.

Forecast

How everything cools and calms, how it all
tones down; how recall and forgetting
feel much the same: how the full
moon tints itself orange for a storm
as strength builds through my own right arm
pointlessly, now its fighting days are gone,
put back like everything else, and forgotten.
I hold on to you with both arms
as the rain scatters and settles in:
how everything cools and calms;
how it all tones down.

Flex

It is not the man within:
what you see when you see
the muscles through my skin
is more and less than me,

so touchy to assay
its temper and my mood,
and itching now to flay
itself, a thing of blood,

the muscle-man will walk
out of his envelope
to bad dreams with no talk
as a bunched and turning rope

that strangles, if it wants,
and squeezes to the bone
the brittle thing it haunts,
and the soft stuff within,

the will to stretch or push
feeding itself through miles
of sinew, and the lush
fibre of pumping cells,

that can neither see nor care,
can only move,
cannot cry in despair
or joy, or cry for love,

but go to their one end
without pause or dissent,
past lover and past friend,
to each indifferent.

The Walk

Boundless east wind
from an empty plain;
sleet rakes the water
over itself, and back in;
the sky is a theatre
of storm- and sunlight,
long jagged cuts
of diamond in slate,

and nobody has stood
long upright, under
that sky, who did not go
down with heavy
steps on heavy steps,
with pain
like a bundle of stones,
into the fast river,

and walk, as walk he must,
breathing the dense and rainy
flat slaps of the air,
out to the very centre
of a rising flood
where it clings and cuts
with cold: it has been
a terror to many.

Quis Separabit

A drive along Belfast's eastern strip
on the home leg of an airport run
at lunchtime, and in blinding rain:
the windscreen's simple weep and wipe,

the roads, the houses, the estates,
all blurred and darkened, out of shape.
The rain, the steady wipe and weep,
brings half in focus, then distorts

Dundonald, and high Castlereagh,
traffic in its long runs below,
with Stormont always just in view
– a smudge of white, of white and grey –

and then the Braniel's show of flags:
as I speed past, I leave behind
an Ulster flag, Ulster's red hand
drenched up there as it slaps and flaps,

beside it – clear as day – the Star
of David, staunch beneath black skies,
flown in defiance where it flies
glaring into the backward mirror,

surviving as one mote of white
lodged like a flaw behind the eyes –
white edged with blue. The message is
a downright question: who will part

blood from blood, and who desert us,
daring to stand here, while we stand?
The road loops back, and has no end.
Here we remain, and who shall part us?

Late Morning

No sign of me.
                    The thaw
as yet hardly begun,

and sunlight leaking through
a picture of the sun
in puddles blocked with ice;

the melt-water collecting
gradually; snow-crust
broken apart with grass:

I might have been a ghost,
a shadow, and not the guest
they had been expecting.

The Pieces

Tail-feathers on the kitchen floor;
up on the rooflight, against the glass,
breast down
                    caught as it floats away.

★

Less than an inch
from the window-flowers
bees all morning
fiddle and bump.

★

The swatted fly had come
to tell us something; now,
instead, it sees the other world
maybe it saved us from.

★

Soft resin, or gum.
Pale amber-coloured tubs
of beeswax in the sun,
unmelting by a miracle
one by one.

★

The heavy traffic
          slow enough
to see drivers' faces,
          all of them

– we were really here,
we looked like this –

far from here
far from this

Music inside the car
is years away.

*

Behind the glass
and in front of the glass
there are other worlds;

sprays of blossom
open themselves

and glare out through the glass.

*

The flowers are far off and vivid
in blasts of sun, sheeted
reflections
all the colours
of gold and bronze.

*

Hot as a bread-oven
all summer every year
the building stood firm
in its squared form
of beeswax and feathers.

*

The otherworldly gnat:
pressed down
to its last breath.

*

Walls made of bronze, imagine,
not buckling under their own weight
but kept upright
by pillars, themselves made of bronze.

*

Fluff-feathers drift up to the ceiling.

*

Slow in arriving, here it is
at last,
and the freesias know,
and the window-glass, with its
warps and smears, that sees everything,
knows all about this:
                    here it is,
much as predicted, at last.

*

They were golden, but not statues,
and they sang, but not with voices
as we knew or had imagined them:
in some lights
birds with long necks,
perched over the bronze walls,
in others, a burn and blur
of gold on the bronze,

and when they sang, it was the gold that sang.

*

Love strengthening in age;
the sun, mid-afternoon,
wants to hold on.
          And the fear of death:
the extinguished

gnat, fly, buzz-bug,
far from here
          knows all this.

★

Bird's feathers
          and no bird
– a vanishing act – gone
like the feathery house
stuck together with wax
that the winds lifted
                    and took away.

★

To listen and listen
to that voice, those voices,
until you die
                    a stranger
with your heart pinned
up where it shouldn't be:
think of that.

★

– far from lovers,
far from children –

★

It's like this: we
were really here; we looked
like this

– far from this,
far from here –

★

In every facet of his eye,
in every glimmer-glitz,
every separate flare,

the gloom and glare
and glower of that other world.

★

Not here – far from it –
but long brought low
to a mourning drone,
small gnats
            passed down
to the world beneath,
its gold and bronze
and all the songs

silently done with,
silently gone.

★

Years afterwards,
                        for years,
the resolute patrol,
step by step, eyes
on the healed-over ground,
to find and carry off the pieces.

★

Roses, are they,
            and bronze-coloured
freesias in the sun?

            That tiny sound:
the bees' soft head-butts
            on the windowpane.

The Street Called Straight

The ceiling makes itself a low arch
deep in the house, in the house of stone,
where you stoop down, then stand up alone
with the cold of walls that are wet to touch,
and in shadows spotted with candlelight.
What holds on here will not soon let go;

it takes the air and sky, it takes your sight
away, it takes everything: you are blind and slow,
and this is still two thousand years ago,
when the body is just a dead or a dying weight
led in here from the street, the street called Straight,
under dark stones into the pressure of stone.

Bowed down, you have stayed these years, the same
weight, a deep weight, felt here, and sealed;
or else a figure cut from parched light,
seen for a moment when the moment came,
some creature made out of bone and flame,
leaving the cripple and the blind man healed.

Arithmetic

To work it through, the brain is just
two clumsy hands of fingers, thumbs,
or a contraption thick with dust
that still performs the easy sums,

imagines twenty take away
eleven, and divides by three;
takes three away; has dismal play
in asking then, for *a* and *b*

which values make the answer nil?
For now the figures cut across
each other and each day, until
the slow arithmetic of loss

becomes a reflex scarcely strange,
not useful, and unused; just there,
one way the wits can rearrange
themselves for time and disrepair,

for miles clocked up and counted down;
for always having less to say,
when every answer is long known,
and numbers take themselves away.

Vigilantes

They stand guard at the invisible gates,
solid against the dark, with covered faces:
we slow, and drive towards them in first gear
on Saturday nights, coming in from town,
then tell them our business, and who we are.
Behind us, the gates close, and we drive on.

★

Hours ahead of me, you have got up early,
and slipped out to the car, just as night ends:
my bedroom curtains tint first light
as I listen to you start the engine
and drive uphill, out of the estate,
not seeing the closed gates, but being seen.

★

You are somewhere on the far side of those gates,
and now the vigilantes with no faces
are watching as I try to slip out early
through first light, where the darkness ends,
as if I were invisible;
as if my business really were my own.

Ode

Who looks out with an equal mind
to huge and meaningless horizons,
where sea makes one long ridge of surf
over the reefs that circle us
– an enormous pallor in all directions
of oblivion once, oblivion returning
to meet at a point, and meet us there –

who sees all this with an equal mind,
knowing how pointless fear is,
and the wild unimportance of the times,
possesses himself, comes into his own
where the tyrant-postures of a future state
can cut no ice, and the ravenous past
consume no tissue from his heart.
                                                    Who sees

with equable, unflappable regard
his own mind open on both sides,
as if the winds would blow through, and the stars
race through it, and the sea pour through,
is equal to the verdict, long delayed,
that comes round from the past or from the future,
returned unopened, not at this address.

44A

I was trying to recall, and find words for,
the heavy sigh of our front door

pulling shut on its air-spring,
the small, mosquito-high ringing

of a timer-light out in the hall,
and the ox-blood colour of the tiles;

all from my narrow perch abroad
at the very hour you died.

★

In the optician's chair that day
beads of light were sore and dry

as I watched for a puff of air
that would reveal the blood-pressure

inside each open, waiting eye:
the thing is not to flinch, to try

to keep a steady head; I flinched;
we tried again; again I flinched.

★

A winter's day in Woodview Drive,
much like the days when you drove

home through twilight in a Ford
Prefect, and the sunset flared

between its windscreen and the rain;
or the rusty Mini, the sky-blue Austin

eleven-hundred, cars you tended
after their best days had ended.

★

The crazy paving, a foot wide,
never cemented, wobbled outside

our front window, where I found
my balance on one stone, and stood

poised, back to the roughcast wall,
like the boy-king of the Braniel,

with toes, feet, ankles and knees
shifting my own weight in the breeze.

★

It would take the light from your eyes –
I know; and it's hardly a surprise,

it's hardly news: that I should find
cold air at the gable-end

strange, or your face then, full
of the fear of death, terrible;

outside is empty, and goes away
fast as light this winter day.

★

Dead pieces in my life begin
to join up, one by one,

and now the Braniel falls below
my feet; the houses start to go,

as I keep steady in a place
made out of distances and space;

a prodigy of balance, where
the last breath is a breath of air.

The Bees

1

When the last of the sunlight goes,
and shadows stretching from the shade
of trees and bushes, long hedgerows,
join up together to invade
wild grasses and the flat pasture,
turning from shadows into night,
then the bees, scattered far and near,
take notice, and start on their flight
back to those walls and roofs they know,
beehives where their small bodies rest
between the dark and dawn; they go
over the threshold, noisy, fast,
massing in hundreds at the doors,
and pour past into their close cells,
cramming chambers and corridors
while the last of the daylight fails:
sleep silences the working hive
and leaves it quiet as the grave.

2

For bees put no trust in the sky
when storms come up with an east wind,
and seldom venture far away
from their stations when downpours impend:
instead, they draw the water off
and stick close to their city walls
where any flights they take are brief;
as the wind blows and the rain falls
they steady themselves through turbulence
by taking with them little stones
(as frail boats, faced with violence
of gales and tides, take ballast on),
and hold their given course along
the clouds, balanced, and balancing.

3

A wonder, how they reproduce:
without courtship, or lovemaking,
without letting their hearts unloose
nerves and sinews like so much string,
without the agony of birth,
they gather offspring from the leaves
and softer herbs, draw with each breath
pollen and children for the hives,
providing themselves with a fresh
ruler, and tiny citizens,
to take the place of some who crash
against the earth, onto hard stones,
brought level by their single love
for flowers, and honey-vintages
(the glorious legacy they leave
behind them, in trust for the ages),
although the time that waits for them
is short enough, and not beyond
a seventh summer; yet the same
nation and race will soldier on,
deathless in spite of time's attacks,
in cells and palaces of wax.

4

All of these things have given pause
to the bees' watchers and guardians
whenever they ascribe the cause
to some influx, some influence
over and above the natural,
an exhalation from beyond
or an element more ethereal
than air itself – maybe the mind
of God, that strengthens as it runs
in earth and sky, or turns in deep
acres of churning oceans,
in herds of cattle, flocks of sheep,

the wild beasts and the harmless beasts,
in life that feels along a thread
from its first moment to the last,
finishing where it all started,
and never reaching a true end:
this keeps the bees away from death
when, at the last, they all ascend
into the skies they lived beneath,
to fly between undarkened spheres
in heaven, and the many stars.

from Virgil, *Georgics* Book IV

Coda

τοῖσι λάμπει μὲν μένος ἀελίου
τὰν ἐνθάδε νύκτα κάτω

The light of the sun
when the sun has gone
beneath the hills
shines on them all,

but with no dawn
or evening light:
unshadowed white,
one equal noon;

while, edging near
around a hearth,
darkness here
comes up from the earth.

TORCHLIGHT

2011

The Neighbours

In the single-bedroom flat I used to cry the night through
as my mother walked the floor with me, rocked me and fed me
past the small, insensible hours, not to wake the neighbours;
though often upstairs there might be half the Group Theatre
going till daybreak – a tiny, bohemian airpocket:
Jimmy Ellis (in the Group, before *Z Cars*), or Mary O'Malley,
and over from next door, next door but one maybe, George
McCann, Mercy Hunter, John Boyd and the BBC,
talking politics or shop, intrigue or gossip the night through.

But perhaps on this occasion there's only the baby
cutting in and out of silence in a high spare room
where the McCanns have just lodged their visiting poet
who by noon will cross from the Elbow Room to the studios
in Ormeau Avenue, and deliver his talk, unscripted,
on 'Childhood Memories'; whose sleep now, if sleep it is,
remains unbroken through the small, insensible hours
between the whiskey nightcap and a breakfast of whiskey.

The Weather

Weightless to me, the heavy leaves
on a sumach drag down their long stems
ready to fall, and spend their lives
on one inflamed, extravagant
display, when light like the rain teems
over and through them; ruined, pendant,
parading every colour of fire
on a cold day at the edge of winter.

They are like the generations of man
of course, and we knew that; we knew
everything pretty much in advance
about this weather, light like the rain,
the red-gold and the gold tattoo

that dying things can print on ruin
(no ruin, in fact, except their own),
flaring up even as they go down.

The sunshine makes reds virulent
and yellows vibrant with decay;
it's not surprise, more like assent
when they fall, when I let them fall,
to what is fated, in its way,
of which this rain-cleared light makes little,
meaning the day can gleam, can glow:
and not a bad day, as days go.

Singles

Unprotected for the most part, out of their paper sleeves,
and stacked in the sideboard as if it were a jukebox
with all of their nicks and scratches and sharp scores
pressed up together in the plastic-smelling dark,

the singles used to spill out like so many side-plates
once I got started on their daily inspection;
tilting the vinyl into sunlight, and closing one eye,
I squinted across the surface, over a dark

spectrum of grooves and dust, where the smooth run-out
ended at a milled ridge, then the label
in blue or black, with its silver-grey lettering
that I learned by heart, spelling the titles and names

slowly to myself, more certainly each time,
to put together words like Gloria, Anna-Marie,
and whole runs of language in THE HUCKLE-BUCK,
SHE LOVES YOU, or SORRY (I RAN ALL THE WAY),

as I ferried singles across our quiet sitting-room
to the Dansette with its open lid, a spindle
and rubber-plated turntable, ready to play them all
to destruction, till late in the morning, when

the patterned carpet was the map of another world
in some year that's not coming around again,
like the showbands and Them, the Beatles and Jim Reeves,
and THIS BOY, DISTANT DRUMS, or BABY PLEASE DON'T GO.

Reversing Around a Corner

Plato could have handled it: the turns,
half-turns and quarter-turns, the speed
and timing are abstract concerns
to be perfected in your head
before they enter the world of sense
and take you on a perfect course
back and around, intelligence
working with gentleness or force
on your hands and feet, your busy eyes
in that manoeuvre – the very one
I fluffed (to nobody's surprise)
in my first test, and now, umpteen
years later, somehow I get right
exactly, without thinking, here
between your house and a building-site
across the road, in reverse gear
and barely glancing back, at best,
as I point myself the other way
(on what, you tell me, is a test-
route) easily, with enough play
in the wheel to give the look of ease
now it can hardly matter, now
there's no one but myself to please,
and rules, and what the rules allow,
don't figure, now there are times when
nothing is beautiful, or true,
with no great difference between
what I can do and I can't do.

Rainbow Ribbons
1980

At the mid-point of a working day
we are the solitary couple
in the Botanic's upstairs lounge,
I with my sweet Martini, sweetened
with lemonade, where feathers of ice
make little prisms in the glass,
she with the same, as indoor lights
on the thousand and one tight black
curls and ringlets of her hair
create their own fair weather,
tumbling and falling like ribbons.

When we step into a sun-shower,
I press her close to kiss
wet hair that is springy and firm
and turns to a whole dark spectrum
as fast clouds hit and miss
each other over our heads, giving
a light so clear it never goes
back exactly as it was.

The Reeds

On my own now with the lake, lake-water's
suck and slap against a wooden jetty
accompanies the solitary, middle-distance
heron that my eyes follow in its take-off
and heavy flight beyond their farthest reach.

★

I can walk for yards across these narrow planks
and touch the tips of reeds on either side
of me, where they come level with my arms:
the reeds move in the water as they give
under my hands, then come back to their places.

⋆

To see her arms and long wrists in the water,
her fingers slim and definite as reeds,
would be too much, and in the building quiet
admit that now, when nobody can hear,
it might be a relief to scream aloud.

⋆

As I turn towards the interrupted noise
where reeds are parting for me like a sea,
my heron circles back from the far shore,
aloof, but still checking on everything
in the water, to see what is really there.

Green Tea

That morning, when I was half-way
to all the way lost, the clouds
seemed to make way
for more clouds in a busy sky;
the path I wanted was one towards
the town, was it? This was country,
and the more progress I made,
it was more, and not less, countryside.

As I confess how I lust after
fluency, and how I distrust it,
fluent with light
our green tea fills the fragile cups
(I am too early or too late,

retracing, is it, my own steps),
cups that are luminous
with a whole language unknown to us.

A day when nothing really gets done,
when sentences break up, and when
nothing avails
against the clinches, snares and toils
of words that want not to be plain,
is it, or not to be held down,
not held to what I mean:
I mean a day much like this one,

between half-way to utter waste
and all the way, when bits of the past
count as pure loss
against the tea leaves' secret signs,
visible, not readable – unless
to my grandmother and her dead friends
where they sit beyond recall,
cups in hand, in the parlour still.

Boiled, but not boiling, water stains
slowly where now it gives back the
glow of the sun
in a cup that's made of porcelain,
and the leaves settle down exactly
across each other, one on one,
each more than half the way
to all the way askew, awry.

A Pair of Shoes

Pencil strokes shine like pewter or gunmetal
over the flimsy paper where you drew
these empty sneakers for no reason at all,
and I look through
them to your words on the other side
that say so little, I can't decide
how to construe

the precise lines and the shadows you worked out
across those crumply shoes, as if they fell
down together, in freakish window-light
starting to fail
on a day full of rain, when the whole sky
comes down with just itself to see by,
so you can't tell

colours apart from versions of grey and white
in the instant that you're taken by surprise –
a silver flash, wings maybe, with eyesight
not the right size
to see whatever's flying; almost
enough, when in daylight the ghost
opens its eyes.

Oxford Poetry

in memory of Mick Imlah

1

You weren't there, but your typescript had arrived
an hour before the copy went to press:
one of us took a bus up the Cowley Road
to get the piece of paper to the printers,
a sheet where every other line was stiff
with Tippex, and over the patches your own hand,
elegant even there, even in biro.
The finished magazines would be wheeled down
in a shopping trolley all the way to Magdalen,
and where they went from there I never knew,
preoccupied with typos I might find,
too late to fix, in something on my watch.
I was the careless one, and still am careless,
for whom your nickname, which was maybe half-
affectionate, of 'Supermac' was apt,
satirically two decades out of date
(I'd told you about how I sent the real
Harold Macmillan gently off to sleep
by spouting verse in the Sheldonian).

I missed things, often. It wasn't until
one afternoon with you, deep in the Chequers,
at a sunny table, drinking like we meant it,
when we were joined by an ancient, fugitive
Glaswegian who talked rubbish for an hour,
and my accent softened, and your open smile
broadened and shone, accepting, that I knew
my stupid blunder in taking you for English.
We weren't in Oxford, even though we sat
in High Street – not *that* Oxford, anyway,
where power hatches and speaks to itself:
we were at home in feeling far from home,
and listening to a voice that wasn't ours,

while in the sunlight I could see you make
connections and corrections both at once.
The blunders of a quarter century
all felt like nothing once I stood apart,
a year ago today, watching them wheel
you out from Magdalen, when you weren't there.

2
13 March, 1972

A typist has got it wrong, and so in pen
the Foreign Secretary corrects his memo,
adding the phrase she left out from his last
sentence of para. 1, in which 'Our own
parliamentary history is one long story
of trouble' is missing three vital words:
he dashes in *with the Irish*, and now it's clear.

The rest is all right: he tells the PM
how they (the Northern Irish) 'are not like
the Scots or Welsh', he tells him how he doubts
they ever will be, how the British interest
is not served best by 'tying them closer
to the United Kingdom'; he recommends
pushing them now towards a United Ireland.

He is himself a Scot: Eton and Oxford
(3rd Class in Modern History), a life
given largely to service, and being spent so now,
adding the weight of his practised signature
as he sends the paper on to Downing Street
like a coda to one long story of trouble
from Alec Douglas-Home (a Christ Church man).

3

Trip-switches tripping, rooms and rooms of them;
all the connections failing one by one;
power and poetry riddled with each other:
the information, accurate and mad,
of a spent lifetime, what does it come to?
One kind of answer is a bare report,
its commentary an open smile – yours;
then a thousand lightbulbs switching themselves off.

The Interruption

Somebody almost takes the call
just when a phone stops, their slow
story reaching the point, maybe,
while three or four others vacantly
wait for the spirit to move: but now
a story with nobody in it
barges straight in, in a flash,
before they can make themselves heard
or finish, before they can start.

Nobody says another word
as all of them hear the silence start;
they just take stock as if, oh,
they see now, and their faces fall.

August, 1998

Draught

He runs cold water into a glass
where he stands in the Braniel kitchen
at the sink, just home from work,

and raises that glass to his stubbled lips
and drinks, and drinks it down in one;
a good draught, he says, of Adam's ale.

★

The kitchen where I can reach the tap
with a long tumbler that came free
from the Maxol station at Gilnahirk

and top up the glass with barley water
then balance it back to head-height,
pausing before the first big gulp.

★

No more than once a week, he takes
the car down to McGowan's for
ten shillings' worth of petrol, waits

as the lad at the pumps goes to fetch
free cutlery (a knife, a spoon)
or glassware; Green Shield stamps.

★

Light from the backyard brings to life
that pale grey liquid in my glass,
and shows how little things have settled;

I watch the turns and twists, like dust-
motes, of all the sunned-on barley-
flecks suspended in the water.

⋆

When I swallow, sometimes there's a long
moment when all the drink is cold
in my chest, when it's a cold hand

laid on my breastbone, and the odd
time when the water fills me up
past any thirst that it can quench.

Canopic Jars

1
Lights

When they had done their job
of making good the air
I breathed, with a last sob
these lungs, that couldn't bear
my weight, gave up on me;
they had emptied themselves out
of speech and secrecy,
of confidence and doubt;
now they could give no more:
silence was really death,
surface really the core;
the soul was really breath.

2
Liver

Hidden again from view,
this organ is at rest
from the thing it had to do
unheeded, unaddressed,
a lifetime long; no more
to work with blood and bile,

here it is deep in store
like an unconsulted file
padded with lost routine,
long past the moment now
when perhaps there might have been
some use for it, somehow.

3
Intestines

Rewound here, and closed in,
these yards of underground
cabling can begin
to turn themselves around
one last time, and as if
they knew what they had done
digesting all that life
slowly, but by the ton,
they must, they can, give up:
just to support a man
who took, from plate and cup,
from jug, oven, or pan
all he could touch or taste,
they made from what he tried
and the small lives that died
in tens of thousands, waste.

4
[Heart]

This jar contains my heart:
when it had beaten its last,
they placed it here apart
from me, or from what passed
for me, as a special case –
unlike Egyptians, who
would keep the heart in place
beneath linen and glue

inside a corpse's chest
to be a quickened seed
as the body rose again,
convinced these were the best
pains to have taken when,
really, there was no need.

Slowest

When the first rockets tore
in at an angle
they left behind nothing
but concrete and steel,

flowers, and weeds flowering
over the bitter soil.
After four years, my
first flowers of jasmine

take me by surprise,
five-petalled, weightless,
and all but forgotten
in this dust-heavy garden,

yet their perfume identical
to what I remember
in the marble and worked stones
slowly persisting

close to the sea,
where jasmine curled up
with weeds and wild roses
one evening in Tyre.

Portrush

I don't know if they ever met in life,
but today the spirits of two dead poets
keep us company as we dash through rain
all the way from the West Strand into town;
Jimmy is about forty, his wild hair
fighting the elements; Archie is wearing
an enormous pullover made for the north,
conspicuous still as the only black man
about here: it rains so hard that our scalps
and our backs ache with it, as Jimmy dodges
quickly into the Northern Counties Hotel
(which isn't here any more) to have a last one,
and Archie heads for that Chinese restaurant
where he brought me once a lifetime ago.
But I'm not able to perform introductions
– Archie I met the once, Jimmy I hadn't
seen for a dozen years before he died
(I owed him better, and neglected him) –
and you and I are shocked by the brutal downpour
plastering us when we've only stopped for chips,
for which, now we're here, we don't have the heart.

Later

But for the time, I would tell you
about a garden in Gilnahirk
(above the road, where you drive through
every morning to get to work),
a garden not there any more
around the red-brick council cottage
kept up by Ruby and James Moore,
where flowers flowered over the edge
of a steep path, over the walls
and into each other's beds; where lines
of bright, new-planted annuals

criss-crossed and trespassed from their lanes
all summer; where the roses flared
and flaunted along trellises, and where
a row of vegetables was cleared
of weeds each morning; a place for sheer
toil in a builder's few spare hours,
working the ground for food and show,
the gable wall a wall of flowers,
the glen in darkness far below:
and I would tell you everything
about that garden, now the land
has been churned up and cleared, to bring
a chip shop and a second-hand
tyre depot, now that it's all gone,
now James and Ruby are in their grave
at Comber, tell you every one
of the flowers I used to pick and save
from flowerbeds filled up to the brim
and over it, but for the time.

Augury

A sound from above like ripped material,
but the bright level clouds are nearly too bright
for me to see what's moving there, the small
dagger-stabs and arrows of birds in flight,
hurling themselves, and pausing, and shooting by:
a dozen swifts unravelling the sky.

A Castaway

When he was washed up naked on the shore
Odysseus improvised a suit of leaves
and clothed himself in that: with nothing more
to lose, with nothing to conceal from thieves,

in one sense, if no other, he was free:
the ground was moving still with the waves' sway;
all his belongings were across the sea
and unimaginably far away;

his body, in the glare of early sun,
was solid, battered, with scars everywhere,
and his face, where so much salt water had run,
was creased to the touch, fragile in the air;

his arms, that lately held a woman close
and hooped her waist, and pressed her to the bed,
the hands that touched her where and how he chose,
that stroked her breasts, and felt her lips, now bled

where splintered wood and rocks in a great storm
had torn them; right down to his shoulders hung
the straggly hair, brittle with salt; his form
in its sand-shadow was bent, no longer young,

for he could not see himself as she had seen him,
although she knew he was a mortal man,
and he searched for fresh water that would clean him,
washing the sea from him, and the leathery tan,

but nothing now could rinse away the years
that clung to him, or those pains his body kept
close as its welts and bruises, close as hairs
on his strong chest, where Penelope had slept.

The Difference

Resourceful as he was, he seemed destined
to be always at the mercy of some
fate or other, his wily spirit twinned
with a targeted body, lashed and battered numb

by the sea, or whatever made the sea move
against him resolutely, tirelessly,
and put him always at one further remove
from the far island where his home might be;

now wet sand with its lines of twigs and stones
like fragments of an indecipherable text,
feathers and shells, seaweed and cast-off bones
wherever one wave stood in for the next

said nothing on this earth is a substitute
for anything else (warm light, a dab of rain,
the tide advancing backwards foot by foot,
flowers in the dunes not coming back again),

so he stared at the face of a faceless ocean
which never would hold still or clarify,
dark to look at, but flashing back the sun
like wine pouring itself out endlessly,

alone with all his plans and his misfortunes
distinct in the light and untranslatable,
knowing himself to be what he thought once
absurd, a man whose cunning and sharp will

were useless, and for all his intelligence
a prisoner in his own life, with no key
or no lock to turn: it was the difference
between the sea and his words for the sea.

The Harbour

Later, he thought about all the disguises
that worked for long enough to do the job,
the dirt and a tattered coat just compromises
with how things might be, once the seasons rob

someone of all their human shape and height,
no matter how upright they were or brave,
tear them with hunger, sap them of all fight,
and set them destitute beside the grave;

those roles of his, and all the assumed names,
details of lives that he could still recall
but never lived, life-stories that made games
from people who were never him at all

seemed less important now, now he was back
at some point after the whole story ended,
only himself again, on that worn track
between town and the harbour, with clothes mended

like his bones, searching the skyline all day
but seeing only sunlight over the waves,
odd shapes on water coming or going away,
never those shore-spirits from sandy caves

or girls standing beside freshwater springs
in conversation, watching him from afar
– nymphs, as it turned out – never those things
that had made his story from mischance and war

larger than any life he could design
out of his own experience and wit,
and never the goddess: the goddess who, when
you see her face, you can't imagine it.

Penalty

The clouds are blue with electricity and rain.
I have bared my head, and walk in a clammy afternoon
with purpose, quickly, skin and clothes stuck with sweat,
like someone searching for treasure, or for a lost child,
desperate under this watchful, unanswering sky;
leaves turning here all point in a single direction
as something touches faintly the hairs on my arms and legs:
it lifts hairs on my shoulders, hairs on my chest,
but without laying hands on me, my unclean flesh
slickened and used and tired, and sore and very old,
that watches out now for a first glance of lightning,
not knowing when or from where it will come, but knowing
that wisdom is to expect death, and fear the goddess.
The clouds are blue with electricity and rain.

Hymn

Greek, sixth century BC

This is about Demeter, the long-haired goddess
Demeter, and about her child, a skinny-legged
little girl who was just taken away
one morning by Hades, Death himself, on the say-so
of his brother Zeus, the deep- and wide-bellowing God.

She was apart from her mother, and from Demeter's
protecting sword, made all of gold, when he came;
she was running about in an uncut spring meadow
with her friends, the daughters of the god Ocean,
and picking flowers here and there – crocuses and wild roses,
with violets and tiny irises, then hyacinths
and one narcissus planted there by Gaia, the Earth,
as Zeus demanded, and as a favour to Death,
to trap the girl, whose own eyes were as small and bright
as the buds of flowers: it blazed and shone out
with astonishing colours, a prodigy as much for

the immortal gods as for people who die.
A hundred flower-heads sprung from the root
with a sweet smell so heavy and overpowering
that the wide sky and the earth, even the salt waves
of the sea lit up, as though they were all smiling.
The girl was dazzled; she reached out with both hands
to gather up the brilliant thing; but then the earth
opened, the earth's surface with its level roads
buckled, there on the plain of Nysa, and up from below
rushed at her, driving his horses, the king of the dead.

He snatched her up, struggling, and he drove her away
in his golden chariot as she wailed and shrieked
and called out loud to her father to help her,
to Zeus, the highest of high powers;
yet nobody – not one god, not one human being,
not even the laden olive-trees – paid heed to her;
but from deep in a cave, the young night-goddess
Hecate, Perses' daughter, in her white linen veil,
could hear the child's cries; and so could the god Helios
– god of the Sun, like his father Hyperion –
hear the girl screaming for help to Zeus, her own father:
Zeus, who was keeping his distance, apart from the gods,
busy in a temple, taking stock there of the fine
offerings and the prayers of mortal men.

For all her struggling, it was with the connivance of Zeus
that this prince of the teeming dark, the god with many titles,
her own uncle, with his team of unstoppable horses
took away the little girl: she, as long as she kept in sight
the earth and the starry night sky, the sun's day-beams
and the seas pulled by tides and swimming in fish,
still hoped, hoped even now to see her mother again
and get back to her family of the eternal gods.

From the mountain tops to the bottom of the sea, her voice
echoed, a goddess's voice; and, when her mother heard
those cries, pain suddenly jabbed at her heart: she tore
in two the veil that covered her perfumed hair,
threw a dark shawl across her shoulders, and shot

out like a bird across dry land and water,
frantic to search; but nobody – neither god, nor human –
was ready to tell her what had happened, not even
a solitary bird would give Demeter the news.
For nine whole days, with a blazing torch in each hand,
the goddess roamed the earth, not touching, in her grief,
either the gods' food or their drink, ambrosia or nectar,
and not stopping even to splash her skin with water.

On the tenth day, at the first blink of dawn, Hecate
came to help her, carrying torches of her own,
and gave her first what news she could: 'Royal Demeter,
bringer of seasons, and all the gifts the seasons bring,
what god in heaven, or what man on this earth
can have snatched away Persephone, and broken your heart?
I heard the sound of her crying, but I couldn't see
who it was; I'm telling you everything I know.'
Hecate said this, and received not one word in reply:
instead, Demeter rushed her away, and the pair of them
soon reached Helios, the watcher of gods and men.

Demeter stopped by his horses, and spoke to him from there.
'If ever I have pleased you, Helios, or if ever
I have done you a favour, do this one for me now:
my daughter's voice was lost on the trackless air,
shrill with distress; I heard, but looked and saw nothing.
You gaze down all day from the broad sky,
and see everything on dry land and the ocean:
so if you have seen who forced away my child
from me, and who went off with her, whether
a man or a god, please, quickly, just tell me.'
She said this, and the son of Hyperion replied:
'Holy Demeter, daughter of Rhea with her long hair,
you are going to hear it all – for I think highly
of you and, yes, I pity you, grieving as you are
for the loss of your skinny-legged little girl. So:
of all the immortal gods, none other is responsible
than the master of the clouds, Zeus himself, who gave her
to Hades his brother to call his own
as a beautiful wife. Hades with his team of horses

snatched her, and dragged her to the thickening dark
as she cried and cried. But come now; you are a goddess:
call an end to this huge sorrow; be reasonable:
there is no need for such uncontrollable rage.
Hades, the lord of millions, is hardly, after all,
the worst son-in-law amongst the immortals,
and he is your own flesh and blood, your own brother.
As for his position – well, he has what was allotted
originally, when things were split three ways,
the master of those amongst whom he dwells.'

So saying, Helios took up the reins, and his horses
were away all at once, bearing up the chariot
like birds with slender wings. And now grief fastened
– a harsher, a more dreadful pain – at Demeter's heart.
Furious with the black cloud-god, the son of Cronos,
she abandoned the gods' city, and high Olympus,
to travel through rich fields and the towns of men,
changing her face, wiping all its beauty away,
so that nobody, neither man nor woman, when
they saw her could recognise her for a goddess.
She wandered a long time, until she came to the home
at Eleusis of the good man Celeus, master there.

Heartsore, heart-sorry, Demeter stopped by the roadside
at the well they called the Maiden's Well, where people
from the town would come for water; sat in the shade
cast over her by heavy branches of olive,
and looked for all the world like a very old lady,
one long past childbearing or the gifts of love,
just like a nurse who might care for the children
of royalty, or a housekeeper in their busy house.
The daughters of Celeus caught sight of her as they came
that way to draw water, and carry it back
to their father's place in great big pitchers of bronze:
Callidice and Clisidice, beautiful Demo
and Callithoe, the eldest girl of all four,
more like goddesses in the first flower of youth.
They had no idea who she was – it's hard for people
to recognise gods – so they came straight up to her

and demanded, 'Madam, where have you come from
and who, of all the old women here, are you?
Why is it that you've walked out past the town
and don't go to its houses? Plenty of ladies
the same age as you, and others who are younger,
are there now, in buildings sheltered from the heat,
to welcome you with a kind word and a kind turn.'

When they had done, the royal goddess replied:
'Good day to you, girls, whoever you may be;
I'll tell you what you want to know, for it's surely
not wrong, when you're asked, to explain the truth.
I am called Grace – my mother gave me that name –
and I have travelled on the broad back of the sea
all the way from Crete – not wanting to, but forced
to make the journey by men who had snatched me,
gangsters, all of them. In that fast ship of theirs
they put in at Thoricos, where the women
disembarked together, and they themselves began
making their supper down by the stern cables.
But I had no appetite for any meal that they made,
and when their backs were turned I disappeared
into dark country, and escaped from those men
before they could sell me, stolen goods, at a
good price, bullies and fixers that they were.
That's how I arrived like a vagrant, and I
don't know what country it is, or who lives here.
May the gods who have their homes on Olympus
send you good husbands and plenty of children
to please the parents; but now, spare a thought
for me, like the well brought-up girls that you are,
and maybe I can come to one of your houses
to do some honest work for the ladies and gentlemen
living there, the kind of thing a woman of my age
does best: I can nurse a new baby, and hold
him safe in my arms; I can keep the place clean;
I can make up the master's bed in a corner
of the great bedchamber, and give all the right
instructions to serving women in the house.'

It was the goddess who said this; immediately
the girl Callidice, loveliest of Celeus' daughters,
spoke back to her, calling her Grandma, and saying:
'Whatever the gods give, however grievous the hardship,
people put up with it, as they must, for the gods
are that much stronger: it's just how things are.
But something I can do is tell you the names
of men who have power and prestige in this town,
who keep its walls in good shape, whose decisions
count for much, and whose advice is listened to here:
wise Triptolemus and Diocles, that good man
Eumolpus, then Polyxeinus, and Dolichus,
and our own dear father of course, all have
wives kept busy with the care of their houses;
not one of them would take a dislike to you
and turn you away from the door – they would welcome
you in, for there *is* something special about you.
Stay here, if you will, and we'll all run back
to tell our mother, Metaneira, the whole story,
then see whether she'll suggest that you come
to ours, and not go looking for another home.
She has a new baby in the house now, a son
born later in life, hoped for and prayed for:
if you were to take care of him, and see him through
to manhood, you would be the envy of any
woman, so well would that childcare be paid.'

Demeter simply nodded her head, and the girls
filled their shiny pitchers up with fresh water
and carried them away, their heads held high.
Soon they were at the family home, where they told
their mother all they had seen, all they had heard.
She ordered them to hurry back, and request this woman
to come and work for a good wage. So then
like deer, or like young calves in springtime,
happy and well-fed, running around in the fields,
they pulled up the folds of their long dresses
and dashed down the cart-track: the long hair,
yellow as saffron, streamed back over their shoulders.
They found Demeter where they had left her, by the road,

and they led her then towards their father's house
while she walked a little way behind, troubled at heart,
her head veiled, and with the dark dress fluttering
this way and that over her slender legs.

They got back to Celeus' house, and went in
through the hallway, where their mother was waiting,
seated by a pillar that held up the strong roof,
with her child, the new son and heir, at her breast.
The girls ran straight to her: slowly Demeter placed
a foot over the threshold, her head touched the rafters,
and around her the entire doorway lit up.
Astonishment and draining fear together shook
Metaneira; she gave up her couch to the visitor
and invited her to sit. But Demeter, who brings
the seasons round, and brings gifts with the seasons,
had no wish to relax on that royal couch, and she
maintained her silence, with eyes fixed on the floor,
until Iambe came up, mindful of her duty,
and offered a low stool, which she had covered
with a sheep's white fleece. The goddess
sat down now, and with one hand she drew
the veil across her face; and there she remained,
sunk in her quiet grief, giving to no one
so much as a word or a sign, sitting on there
without a smile, accepting neither food nor drink
for an age, as she pined for her beautiful daughter,
until Iambe, resourceful as ever, took
her mind off things with jokes and funny stories,
making her smile first, then laugh, and feel better,
and Metaneira offered her the cup she had filled
with wine, sweet as honey: but she shook her head
and announced that, for her, it was not proper now
to take wine – instead, she asked Metaneira
to give her some barley-water and pennyroyal
mixed up together: the queen made this, and served it
to the great goddess, to Demeter,
who accepted it solemnly, and drank it down.
Only then did Metaneira begin to speak:
'Madam, you are welcome here; all the more so

for coming from no ordinary stock
but, I'd say, from the best – for your every glance
is full of modesty and grace, you have something
almost royal about you. But what the gods give us,
hard though it is, we mere human beings
endure: all our necks are under that yoke.
You are here now, and whatever is mine shall be yours.
This little boy – my last born, scarcely hoped for,
granted me by the gods only after much prayer –
nurse him for me now, and if you raise him
to be a healthy, strong man, then any woman
at all will be jealous to see you, so great
will be the reward I give you for your work.'
Demeter replied: 'Accept my greetings, good lady,
and may the gods be kind to you. I will indeed
take care of this fine boy of yours, as you ask.
I shall rear him, and neglect nothing: sudden sickness
will never harm him, and never will some witch
of the forest, who taps roots for magic or poison,
touch a single hair of his head; for I know
stronger sources to tap, and I know the remedy
for all such assaults: a sure one, unfailing.'

Then with her two arms, the arms of a goddess,
she drew the baby in close to her own bosom,
and its mother smiled at the sight. In the big house
from then on Demeter looked after the son
of Celeus and Metaneira, while he grew up
at a god's rate, not eating solids, or taking
milk, but fed by her with ambrosia, as if
he were indeed a god, born of a god;
she breathed gently over him and kept him close,
and at night, unknown to anyone, she smuggled him
into the burning fire, like a new log of wood.
He was thriving so well, and looking so much more
than a human child, that both the parents were amazed.

And the goddess Demeter would have delivered him
from age and from death, had not Metaneira
been up one night and, without so much as

giving it a thought, from her own bedroom
looked into the hall: in sheer terror for the child
she screamed, and did her best to raise the alarm,
seeing the worst and believing it; she called out
to her little boy, half-keening: 'Demophoön,
my own baby, this stranger is hiding you
in the big fire, she's the one making my voice shrill
with pain, Demophoön, my darling, my child.'

She cried all this out, and the goddess heard her.
Furious that instant, mighty Demeter
took the child – their last born, scarcely hoped for –
and with her own immortal hands she brought him
out of the fire, set him gently on the floor,
then, brimming with anger, turned on Metaneira:
'You stupid creatures, you witless and ignorant
humans, blind to the good as well as the bad
things in store for you, and no use to each other:
I swear to you here, as gods do, by the rippling
dark waters of Styx, that I would have made
this child of yours immortal, honoured, a man
untouched by age for eternity; but nothing now
can keep the years back, or keep death from him.
There is one mark of honour that will always be his:
because he once slept in my arms, and lay in my lap,
all the young men at Eleusis, at the set time
each year, as their scared duty, will gather
for the sham fight, and stage that battle forever.
For I am Demeter, proud of my own honours
as the bringer of joy to the gods, and of blessings
to mortal men. Everyone now has to build me
a spacious temple, with its altar underneath,
by the steep walls of your city, where a hill
rises just above the Maidens' Well. The rites
will be as I instruct, when I teach you the ways
to calm my anger, and be good servants to me.'

And with that, instantly the goddess changed form –
her height, her whole appearance – shuffling away
old age, so that sheer beauty blazed and spread

in and around her; from her robes a gorgeous perfume
drifted, and from her immortal flesh there came
pure light, with the reach of moonbeams; her hair
flashed over her shoulders, and the entire house
was flooded with a sudden brilliance of lightning
as she stepped out through the hall. Metaneira's
knees went from beneath her, and for an age
she sat there speechless, not even thinking
to pick that dear child of hers up from the floor.

When his sisters heard the boy starting to cry
they jumped straight out of their beds, and one
caught him up in her arms, and held him close,
while another stoked the fire, and a third
dashed on bare feet to take hold of her mother
and help her away. As the girls huddled round him,
trying to comfort him and dab his skin clean,
the baby wriggled and fretted, knowing full well
these nurses were hardly the kind he was used to.

That whole night long, shaking with fear, the women
did their best to appease the great goddess.
When dawn came at last, they told everything
to Celeus, exactly as Demeter had instructed,
and he, as their ruler, lost no time
in calling the citizens together, and giving them
the order to build this goddess her temple
and to put her altar just where the hill rises.
They listened to him, and they did all that he said,
so that a temple rose up, as the goddess required.
When the job was done, and the people stopped working,
they all went home; but golden Demeter
installed herself in her temple, apart from the other gods,
and stayed there, eaten up with grief for her daughter.

She made that year the worst for people living
on the good earth, the worst and the hardest: not one
little seed could poke its head up from the soil,
for Demeter had smothered them all; the oxen
broke their ploughs and twisted them, scraping

across hardened furrows; and all the white barley
that year was sown in vain. She would have destroyed
every single human being in the world
with this famine, just to spite the gods on Olympus,
had not Zeus decided to intervene: first
he dispatched Iris, on her wings the colour of gold,
to give Demeter his orders, and she did as he asked,
covering the distance in no time, and landing
at Eleusis, where the air was filled with incense.
She found Demeter wearing dark robes in the temple,
and spoke to her urgently: 'Zeus, our father
who knows everything, summons you back now
to join the family of the immortal gods:
come quick, don't let his command be in vain.'
But her pleas had no effect at all on Demeter:
then Zeus sent out all of the gods, one by one,
to deliver his summons, bringing the best of gifts,
with whatever fresh honours she might desire;
but Demeter was so furious then that she
dismissed every speech out of hand, and told them all
that she would neither set foot again
on Olympus, nor let anything grow on the earth,
unless she could see her beautiful daughter once more.

When he heard this, Zeus, the deep- and wide-bellowing God,
sent Hermes with his golden staff down into the dark
to talk to Hades there, and ask his permission
to lead Persephone back up from the shadows
and into daylight again, where her mother
could set eyes on her, and so be angry no longer.
Hermes agreed to do this: he hurried away
from his place on Olympus, down into the earth's
crevasses and crannies, down, till he reached
the king of all the dead in his underground palace,
stretched out at his ease, and by his arm a trembling
bride, who pined still for the mother she had lost.
Coming up close to him, the god Hermes began:
'Hades, dark-haired lord and master of the dead,
my father Zeus orders me now to take away
from Erebus the royal Persephone, back

to the world, so that Demeter, when she sees
with her own eyes her daughter returning
may relent, and give up her implacable grudge
against the gods – for what she now intends
is terrible, to wipe from the face of the earth
the whole defenceless species of mortal men
by keeping crops under the ground, and then starving
heaven of its offerings. In her rage, Demeter
will have nothing to do with the gods, and she sits
closed in her own temple, apart, holding sway
there over the rocky citadel of Eleusis.'

Hades listened, with just the hint of a smile
on his face, but did not disobey the express
order of Zeus the king, and he spoke at once:
'Go, Persephone, go back now to your mother,
go in good spirits, and full of happiness,
but don't feel too much anger or resentment.
You know, I won't be the worst of all the gods
to have for a husband, brother to your father Zeus;
and here you could be the mistress of everything
that lives and moves, have the finest of honours
among the gods, while for all those failing to pay
their dues by keeping you happy with sacrifice,
proper respect and generous gifts, there will be
nothing in store but punishment for ever.'

Persephone jumped straight up, full of excitement,
when she heard what he said; but Hades, looking
around him, and then back over his shoulder,
gave her the tiny, sweet seed of a pomegranate
for something to eat, so that she would not stay
up there forever with the goddess Demeter.
Then Hades got ready his gold-covered chariot,
hitching up his own horses, and in stepped
Persephone, with the strong god Hermes beside her,
who took the reins and the whip in his hands
as both of the horses shot forward obediently
out and away, making good speed on their journey,
untroubled by the sea, or by flowing rivers,

or grassy glens, or freezing mountain tops:
they sliced thin air beneath them as they flew.

When they came to a stop, it was in front of the temple
where Demeter kept vigil; and, at the sight of them,
she ran forward wildly like someone possessed.
At the sight of her mother, Persephone leapt out
and into her arms, and hugged her, and she wept,
and the two of them, speechless, clung hard
to each other, until suddenly Demeter
sensed something wrong, and broke the embrace.
'My darling,' she said, 'I hope that down there
you didn't eat anything when he took you away?
Tell me, and tell me now: for, if you didn't,
you can stay with me for ever, and with the gods,
and Zeus, your father; but, if you did eat
anything at all, then you'll have to go back
underground for the third part of every year,
spending the rest of the time at my side: when
flowers come up in spring, and bloom in the summer,
you will rise too from the deep mists and darkness –
to the amazement of men, as well as the gods.
But how did Hades abduct you? What tricks
did he use to bring you away to the dark?'
'Mother,' Persephone answered, 'I will tell you it all.
When Hermes came for me on the orders of Zeus,
to take me out of Erebus, so you could see me
and abandon your vendetta against the gods,
I jumped for joy; but then Hades, unnoticed,
gave me the seed of a pomegranate to eat,
and made me taste it: it was sweet like honey.
I'll explain, just as you ask me to, how he
snatched me away in the first place, when Zeus
planned everything to bring me down under the earth.
We were playing together in an uncut meadow
– me and all my friends – and gathering for fun
handfuls of the wild flowers that were growing there:
saffron and irises, hyacinths, and young roses,
lilies gorgeous to look at, and a narcissus
that bloomed, just like a crocus, in the soil.

While I was taken up with that, from nowhere
the ground beneath me split apart, and out
came the great king of millions of the dead
who dragged me, as I screamed, into his gold-
covered chariot, and took me down into the earth.
Now you've heard what it hurts me to remember.'

That whole day long, they were completely at one:
each warmed the other's heart, and eased it of sorrow,
the two of them brimming over with happiness
as they hugged one another for joy again and again.
The goddess Hecate came to them and joined them;
still wearing her veil of white linen, she caught
Demeter's little daughter over and over
in her arms, and became her companion for ever.

Only then did Zeus, the deep- and wide-bellowing God,
send down to speak to Demeter her own mother,
Rhea, to reconcile her with her family.
On his behalf, she could offer whatever new honours
were needed, and guarantee that Persephone
would stay down in the darkness for only a season,
the third of a year, and the rest with her mother
and all of the gods. Rhea hurried to the task,
reaching the fields near Eleusis at Rarion
where harvests once were abundant, but now
no harvest could come up from the cropless plain
where Demeter had hidden away the white barley,
though afterwards, as the spring went on, it would
thicken and move with long corn, and the furrows
would be filled in due course with cut stalks
while all the rest was gathered up into sheaves.

Here the goddess first came down from the trackless air
and she and Demeter greeted one another with joy.
Rhea delivered her message from Zeus, and the promises
he made for Demeter, and for Persephone,
urging her daughter, 'Now, child, you must
do the right thing, and not venture too far
by keeping up this grudge of yours against Zeus:

let food grow again for people on the earth.'
Demeter could say nothing against this: she allowed
crops then and there to come from the fertile ground;
she freighted the wide world with flowers and leaves.

She went then to the men in power – Diocles,
Triptolemus, Eumolpus, and Celeus himself,
the people's leader, to give them instruction
in her liturgy and rites: all of the mysteries
neither to be questioned, nor departed from,
and not to be spoken about for fear of the gods,
a fear so great as to stop every mouth.
Whoever has witnessed these is blessed among men:
whoever has not been inducted, whoever
has taken no part in them, can expect no good
fortune when death fetches him to the darkness.

Once she had revealed all of this, Demeter
returned to Olympus and the company of the gods;
there she and Persephone, holy and powerful,
live beside Zeus himself, where he plays with thunder.
Anyone whom they favour is deeply blessed,
for they send the god Wealth to his own hearth
dispensing affluence to mortal men.

You who protect the people of fragrant Eleusis,
rocky Antron, and Paros surrounded by the sea,
Lady Demeter, mistress, bountiful goddess,
both you and your lovely child Persephone,
favour me for this hymn, give me a living,
and I will heed you in my songs, now and always.

The Wait

They would bury ashes or bodies in the evening,
then say whatever was right to say, looking
out into a bruised and sun-inflamed west
to think of the dead, and take leave of them.
There would be noise from here and there – people,
animals, carts, invisible cicadas –
and the one road to town would darken. When
everyone had gone back, and night came,
the spirit would loiter unseen by its grave,
alone and afraid to go far, anxious
for dawn, and departure then from the earth.

Sappho fr. 58

Children, take your fill of the good things
on offer from every well-dressed Muse,
and each clear note of the singing line:

my own flesh is showing its age; the head
of hair that was dark is dark no more,
and my heart makes heavy work of beating;

knees can barely carry me that once
would keep me dancing like the young deer
quickly, where now I have to draw breath.

Nothing to be done: for there's nobody
who goes on living without getting older –
just as, they say, Tithonus found out

when, crazy about him, the goddess
of dawn, with her rose-pale arms,
took him off to the edge of the earth

still fresh-faced and good-looking, only
for age to claim him in due course, while
his lover neither grew old nor died.

Country

1

I am making believe I
remember this drive-through town,

and the way they see you through
the glass, the way they clock you

(me: I might be related
to half of them) – big boys

recently men, ten or fifteen
years from an early death

who walk between doorways, and seem
to be chewing on their fists

(where the cellphones must be),
not for a single moment

missing me, now I'm back
(Merle Haggard) *I'm right back where*

I've really always been, with flags still
lynched at half-mast from every

other lamppost; driving out of town
in a hire car, with the music on.

2

The hotels were always like this:
light-industrial, bare

and ugly in farmers' fields.
Every weekend, the carvery

(three or four roast meats
rinsed with all-purpose gravy),

men standing at the long bar,
silent; and the Friday

dinner-dances, the weddings
on Saturdays till late.

It's all you can eat,
but I can't eat it,

and instead slow-stare
at a big satellite screen:

I know that I
should leave, but then

I just can't go;
for this is long ago

and still to come;
all different, and the same;

and the football and the races
haven't changed in thirty years.

3

On a hill far away, the masts
for radio and phone traffic, broadcasts

of all kinds, stand upright
together among drizzly clouds,

bearing up their weightless load
of signals in a relay race:

rain and the wind are overwrought
with all they carry, noon and night,

wherever, even in that place.

4

The little roads, signed off
to a townland or a farm

are the ones I turn from
by driving straight ahead,

just tilting my head
to long names of places,

although I am stone-deaf
to – say – the call

of Lungs Mission Hall,
travelling on, graceless,

and making believe
I never felt these hills'

threaded, invisible,
Jesus-wired

forcefields in even
my childhood's blood:

the pain of the Gospel,
that for the truth's sake

will separate, forsake,
part blood from blood,

all of it here still
where Gospel is heartbreak,

a high lonesome wail
for what's gone and to come,

but tired, tired.
This world is not my home.

5

Not here – an ocean away –
but somewhere very like,

the big-eyed eldest son
of 'Colonel' Monero Loudermilk

was born and raised to the hard
earth, then just walked away:

tall Ira Louvin
got drunk, learned mandolin,

got drunk, and sang
fit for heaven

love songs, gospel, *tragic songs
of life*, in high harmony

with his cherub-chopped brother;
got drunk, got Jesus,

and always got drunk again,
half rattlesnake, half man

(and that was according
to his friends), living on

to die in a wrecked car
out on some highway or other –

I didn't hear
nobody pray, dear brother –

who had cursed out his admirer,
the raw Elvis Aaron

to his face after one show
for a 'fuckin' white nigger';

who employed the telephone
cord to strangle his second

wife some, before she left him
her memento, four bullet wounds,

four bullets he carried for life;
who never was safe

to be with, safe or sound;
and who, when *the whiskey*

and blood ran together
went home to his Saviour

between hot-silvery
asphalt and the poor ground.

6

In such a state
that he won't even cross the street,

in Augher, a man my age
stands at the verge

and meets my eyes, I think,
with his tired-out eyes.

The red face is the drink:
he looks without surprise

as I leave him behind;
beyond that, a blank;

and who gives who the slip
is open as the sky,

or now the brisk two-step
(Willie Nelson) of *do you mind*

too much if I
don't understand?

7

So just how sentimental?
About 100%

and don't forget it:
power in the blood

and all the risks of that;
older, and much worse now

than when I upped and fled.
For all over town

the news is out: *soon*
his head

like mine will bow.
The tight air overhead

is jittery, alive
with music and pictures, voices

all scrambled, but not dead,
that pulse through years and places

never remote again,
and here I am *making believe*

I never lost you, a one-two-
one dance time, Patsy Cline

steel-soft, not gone,
the phrasing exact, heartbroken;

my father and my mother
still dancing to it, somewhere;

all that, and the man
on the road I left behind,

bowed, put-upon,
his head like mine.

Riddarholmskyrkan

Against the Baltic Sea
ink-lit from underneath
on that bright evening, we
watched our dispersing breath
and walked over clean stones
to where they kept their dead
kings in a stash of bones
ornate with gilded lead,
carved oak and filigree:
I thought that I could see
in there one polished wreath
made out of wood, that shone
back light from overhead
into the well-kept vault,
but I heard our living steps
that echoed to a halt
no sooner come than gone
diminish and retreat
away out through the gaps
between the sea and town
like some repeating phrase:
I could hear myself repeat
it's not my fault, or *this*
isn't happening, as though
saying would make it so.

Broken

Once I had lost you, you became
a little girl and not a woman,

a little girl who cried and cried
in the dark, as your sobs carried

across land and water; echoed
through my own cries like a chord

of grief and fear, of injustice;
made everywhere one empty space

with you lost in it, lost and scared,
knowing you couldn't be rescued:

so dawn came in with birds lamenting
daylight in their broken songs,

while the walls rang still with your cries,
accusing but defenceless,

for I could give you no comfort or shield,
and your tears were all the tears in the world.

Least

Outside, a light shuffle
where something is moving
away from or around
the house; and that sound –
the half-sound an animal
makes near home, or roving
far from it, a scratch
through twigs, grass and stones,
can leave me this once
unstartled, feeling each
noise as subliminal
work done, unplanned,
an action, for which
I simply don't matter,
not now, and not later,
all perfectly clear, and
no less than the heart's speech
abrupt, minimal.

Childhood Memories

1
The Battery Boy

As our black Ford Prefect rumbled from Stranmillis to the Braniel
on Saturday nights in winter, I looked from the back seat
at young trees in the dark, sodium lights, Belisha beacons
passing behind us through the brightened, sideways rain,
and sometimes caught sight of a solitary night-watchman
in his hut beside roadworks; I even glimpsed his face
glowing from the brazier, red cigarette and kettle
visible for a moment, thin steam from his mug of tea.

You had some name for him, a name that I repeated
with my other chant, *We're nearly home, we're nearly home*,
that lonely man who sat all night by a few coals,
watching, and breaking the dark; a name that I've forgotten,
but get back, nearly, sometimes – like today, when I
pictured a beaming face, all eyes, and called it *Torchy*.

2
1966

The first time I ever saw a man riding a horse
was when the farmer with a red face and a wig
came swaying on his saddle up the Gilnahirk Road,
beneath him the enormous white and grey creature
and coming behind him a fife band, playing *Dolly's Brae*:
I remember his drinker's nose, as well as the bright graffiti
of broken veins scribbling his cheeks, his false
curls of black hair, and the sword upright in front of him.

Aunt Ruby held my hand as we looked down from the garden
where I was frightened and agog, too small to know
that this armed man was not the actual King Billy
riding up to Mann's Corner to claim his own, or that
he would not appear after tea, huge at the parlour door,
when my uncle James recited *The Orange ABC*.

3
Souvenir d'Ypres

It was a good half-century after the battle
that my great-uncle Archie, bedridden, propped-up
to talk to the boy, took one look at my model soldiers
and asked about the shiny, field-grey, moulded man
who lay flat on his stomach, with a rifle levelled
in front of him, taking aim: when I explained he was
a German sniper, Archie held him up, then laughed
and offered only, 'Aye, the snipers, they're the boys!'

I have his pocket-book, embossed A.G., inside it
an old pound note; his childhood copy of Robert Burns;
a swagger-stick, topped with silver, he had in the army,
and a brass cartridge case, the handle for a paper-knife,
marked *Souvenir d'Ypres*: that's all of him, flat out,
smiling, with his bare feet poking from the blanket.

4
Torchlight

Power-cuts in the strike added a new dimension
to the games I was playing with plastic soldiers and tanks
at the back of the sitting-room: now, in the dark,
stealthy commandos started on their midnight raid
to disable a German Panzer and a gun emplacement
under the full moon of a propped electric torch
that shone from high on the settee down to the floor,
lighting up brittle artillery and carpet pile.

Further back, the rest of the furniture was edged
with a penumbra of torchlight – the weakest shine
on a table top, the reflection of a reflection
on curving glass in the dead television screen:
shadows regrouped and shifted, as I crept to war
with the eye of a burning torch burning in my eye.

5
Blue Skies

It must be warm weather, for the front door and the hall
are both open, and I am sitting on the path
watching crowds in a field above the high Braniel
who are themselves listening to an amplified roar
that is Paisley's, unmistakably, and echoes down
this far to Woodview Drive, although his words are lost
in their own noise, and only the outrage and the scorn
come through intact on lazy, slow-dancing thermals.

I start to look instead at an almost cloudless sky,
a blue sky in fact, and I tune the new transistor
to a mixture of midsummer babble and pop music,
cushioned, buoyed up, and floating over the big noises
to *See my Baby Jive* and *Summer (The First Time)*
long after the audience has trickled from the hill.

6
Petrol

I didn't see it, although I heard about it later,
the little gift that entered straight through the front door
early one evening, when everybody was out,
and broke on the cold floor-tiles, the ox-blood tiles,
igniting in the dark for maybe a few seconds
then burning low, then fading completely away
to be found later: scattered bits of a milk-bottle,
heat-stains beneath them; the burned rag, and the smell.

I had to imagine the light it must have given out
as it spurted briefly up the flight of concrete steps
and slapped the walls and sank, then bubbled up again,
coating the red-brown floor with shapes of amber and orange
that sloped and lingered most when I would close my eyes
to press the eyelids with my fingers, all that year.

7
Bits and Pieces

One February night, my father came home shaking
with his face blank, and cold hands, not really speaking,
and although ours was a house that never kept strong drink
he needed more than water to steady him that Monday
after he'd driven from the top of the Castlereagh Road
on to the dual carriageway, where what he saw
was the bombers' car in fragments, then the four of them
scattered in lumps, being scraped up from the pavement.

A little crowd had recourse to the Dave Clark Five
as it chanted at the ambulances and fire engines
over and over the chorus from *Bits and Pieces*, while
by the garage forecourt policemen gleaned the mortal
remains of Steele and Bell, Magee and Dorrian
expertly, having done this kind of thing before.

8
The Collar

On his annual visits from Stranraer, my uncle Tom
(a great-uncle, tall and blind, unstoppable)
would put me to the test: first, it was Bible-stories,
then my catechism, and finally, when I
somehow was learning Greek, my *ho, he, to,*
known from his training days, like the boys' chorus
in the tenements of *Maw, throw us a jeely piece*
that he would bellow, laughing, decades and decades on.

He wore the collar everywhere: once, it had saved
his skin when, with his height and his bare fists,
he stopped the shipyard men lynching a Catholic;
now it got him a good seat in the Martyrs' Memorial
where he said the famous preacher spoke well, but forgot
the imperative, to hate the sin and love the sinner.

9
Kenneth

My grandmother's grave is heaped with roses and carnations
on a dark afternoon in my first flash-photograph,
and behind it, in the drizzle, Mrs Kyle is standing
with her hanky in her hand, friendless, not going home –
home where her son Kenneth might or might not be,
dapper even in his middle years, my father's best man
and like him well turned-out, a touch fastidious
although his good clothes have about them the sheen of age.

As it happens, Kenneth outlives his own mother
by only a year or two: he has fed on whisky
for so long, at the end it sweats from his every pore
and he never comes out. Mrs Kyle grips her handbag
as a flashbulb in its plastic cube erupts and blisters,
coating with light the flowers and their wet cellophane.

10
Spartans

Across the Lisburn Road, every other wall was marked
with big initials, FTP or UVF,
beneath the billboard adverts for *Harp*, *Old Spice: The Mark*
of a Man, or the Confidential Telephone,
and by eight on that hot evening, all the cars
had gone away, leaving a dog or two, and drinkers
quietly threading a course from lounge bar to lounge bar
while down the sidestreets footballs smacked on gable walls.

Messenia was Bradbury Place, and Thermopylae
the narrow cut outside Taughmonagh's tintown
for the Tartan gang who changed themselves from LRT
and crossed over that night as the Lisburn Road Spartans,
surrounding the hall, kicking a door in, breaking
the boy's legs like sticks, and carving his neck with LRS.

11
Saturday

We would leave the band practising noisily at school
and take the long walk down Great Victoria Street
where records might be bought, or looked over, thought about;
then a longer walk, through town, in through the barriers,
having our pockets searched, searching our pockets for change,
and striking out that day to what was left of Smithfield
to pick up some bargain Stevie had got word of:
with nothing for the bus, we trailed back the way we came.

Some RUC men gave us a lift in their armoured car
after the boys at head-level on a parapet
aimed half a dozen kicks, though none of them at me –
at Stevie, with the blood pouring from both nostrils
on his steady walk, and his head still full of music,
cradling a bag of singles as he weighed up the damage.

12
Tommy

He would see you coming half-way up Dunluce Avenue,
and specialised in a long-range, drawn-out 'Well?',
to answer which you had to approach, and go with him
at a painful crawl all the way to the Lisburn Road, where
your two paths could decently diverge; Tommy looked
much older than he was, but there was nothing of him –
unwashed and unshaven, crippled with something, his only
ports of call by then the post-office and the pub.

He stuck to the wrong names for everyone, and he crooned
impenetrable songs to himself; when he died
alone, and the tiny house was cleared then cleaned out,
for months I would still avoid him, see a filthy coat
propped up over a stick, moving, and hear him greet
my mother from a distance with 'Well, Mrs Donnelly?'

This Earth

Whenever I talk to them, they don't answer: maybe
their silence is meant to imply something – that I
should know the answers already – maybe it's just
silence, maybe they can't speak, they don't exist,
and for this job I'm going to need the god Hermes
to walk for me among the undisciplined armies
of the dead, to search out this one and that one
as they wander round without any hurry or reason
and then deliver himself of what I have to say.
He has a sad look, for all his silver skin and his finery,
having been there too often before, a survivor
of glam rock, all metallic spray-painted feathers
and glittery boots, with his make-up peeling
from an age-stricken face; now there's no telling
what music he hears while he looks at the distance
where there's no music at all, and where mischance
is the way of things. If a song can be a present,
I'll give him *Flyin' Shoes* by Townes Van Zandt
(whose ghost, when he's down there, he might well meet,
hungover and good as its word, *I don't think that*
I'm going to benefit from anything on this earth).
I'll offer him whatever all his trouble is worth,
but he's too far gone now even for country music
and mottoes like *Love is just basically heartbreak.*
He clatters away, and I know that he's not coming back.

The Cheetah

1

Cat-shaped, but bigger than a cat,
on its long string the toy balloon
rose and wandered, while you sat
tethering it this afternoon
to your right hand, correcting me
when I misread its spots, and called
the cheetah a leopard: your free
hand pointed where the creature stalled
and started on its leash; you shaped
its profile for me in the air
as you jumped to your feet, escaped
our skyless room, and there you were
outside, and I was with you, saying
not to let go, not to let go,
for fear the cheetah, toppling, swaying,
would leave us standing far below
and helpless: but you laughed and said
that was the whole idea, then
stretched one arm up over your head,
with all the cheetah's lift between
two fingers, and you opened them,
letting it jump high in the wind,
the long string trailing, helium
so light once it was unentwined
that the balloon shot upwards, flew
across the houses, over town,
but kept till it was out of view
the cat-shape of its yellow-brown.

2

You were delighted, and we watched
until the drifting shape was gone
entirely, and the whole sky matched
itself in patchy blue again.
I saw myself drawing a line
in the air around some dangerous
fast-moving predator of mine
that I enclosed, and filled with gas,
to set it loose into the day:
what I held, or was holding to,
could take itself up and away,
and all there was for me to do
was let it go. I almost felt
the string rise and unravel through
my fingers, like someone who knew
that he would give up everything
he had and could have, everything,
to stand here for these minutes, to
search in the empty sky with you;
and I could sense the shiny pelt
of that wild animal ascend
out of my reach for good, to live
without us at the cold, far end
of the harm we do, the hurt we give,
and join the cheetah stalking space,
not to be ours again; to be
a lost shape in some open place
high up: and that's the whole idea.

NOTES AND INDEXES

Notes

This volume includes nearly all of the contents of my five collections of poetry; although the first of these books was published in 1989, the earliest-written pieces here come from the mid-1980s, while the most recent poems in this *Collected* were composed in 2010. Roughly speaking, then, the present book contains a quarter-century of work.

In the texts of the poems generally, I have changed as little as possible. I have, however, made changes to a number of poems in my first two collections, dropped some, and rearranged the order of others. I think my younger self might forgive these intrusions from his middle-aged successor, and perhaps recognise them as coming closer to the books he was intending to write.

Although none of its poems survives into this *Collected*, the selection of my work published in Belfast by The Blackstaff Press in *Trio Poetry 3* (1982) was an important encouragement early on, for which I remain grateful. Just as vital, much later, were the enthusiasm and support I was fortunate to receive from Michael Schmidt and Carcanet Press.

The following notes attempt to record specific debts, and to explain some references. I am well aware of how many other debts of a more personal nature are going unrecorded, and of how curious a return a *Collected Poems* must seem for the investments of all those whose encouragement has been so valuable to me over half my lifetime. I trust that what cannot ever be repaid can still be acknowledged with profound gratitude.

PMcD
Woodstock, Oxfordshire
22 January 2012

Biting the Wax (1989)

p. 18 'Silent Night'

Harold Le Druillenec was arrested by German occupying forces in Jersey, and transported to the Willhelmshaven camp in 1944–5. His experiences there were later used in a radio programme broadcast on the BBC Home Service; this poem draws heavily on the radio script, which is printed in Laurence Gilliam (ed.), *BBC Features* (London, 1950).

p. 29 'The Hands of Juan Peron'

This poem has been moved to its present position from that in *Adam's Dream*, where it was first collected.

p. 31 'The Green, Grassy Slopes of the Boyne'

The title of this poem is the refrain of a popular Northern Irish loyalist marching-song. The Braniel housing estate is a large area of public housing, built in the outskirts of east Belfast in the 1950s. 'Braniel' (from the Irish, *an Braineal*) is pronounced to rhyme with 'Daniel'.

p. 33 'The Third Day'
The opening line of this poem is that of Michael Longley's 'An Image from Propertius' in his *An Exploded View* (1973).

p. 34 'Sunday in Great Tew'

On 8 November 1987, the Provisional IRA murdered twelve, and injured a further sixty-three, of those attending a Remembrance Sunday event at the Cenotaph in Enniskillen, Co. Fermanagh.

Adam's Dream (1996)

p. 63 'Adam's Dream'

This poem quotes from and adapts material from James Lees-Milne, *The Age of Adam* (London, 1949) and John Fleming, *Robert Adam and his Circle in Edinburgh and Rome* (London, 1962).

Pastorals (2004)

p. 71 Epigraph

A literal translation of these two lines of Greek (which were written by a second-century poet called Satyrus), would be: 'Echo sings without a tongue through the fertile meadow, answering the birds with her late-sounding voice.'

p. 73 'Two Trees'

Fraelissa and Fradubio are characters in Edmund Spenser's *The Faerie Queene*, Book I, Canto ii.

p. 74 'The Cup'

This is a translation of part of Theocritus, *Idylls* I; I am indebted to Richard Hunter's edition, *Theocritus: A Selection* (Cambridge, 1999).

p. 80 'The Victory Weekend'

'Friday' quotes from John Dryden's libretto for Henry Purcell, *King Arthur: Or, The British Worthy* (1691), and is indebted to a Royal Opera House production of the piece in May 1995 (dir. Graham Vick).

p. 105 'Hush'

This poem partly translates Giacomo Leopardi's 'L'Infinito'.

p. 112 'Eclogue'

This poem imitates Virgil, *Eclogue* I.

The House of Clay (2007)

p. 130 'War Diary'

The first line of this poem is quoted from Edward Thomas's diary for 1 January–8 April 1917, where it is found on the last pages.

p. 132 'The Other World'

The last line of this poem is a literal translation of a single-line fragment of Pindar (fr. 136a).

p. 146 'In Heaven'

This poem adapts lines from Virgil, *Aeneid* VI, in which Aeneas and the Sibyl, having performed the necessary rites, enter the Elysian fields:

> When they had done all of this, and obeyed the goddess's order,
> At length they came to the joyful country, covered in long grass
> And beautiful, with its holy groves, the retreats of good spirits.
> The air they breathe is larger here, and it clothes with a purple
> Light those meadows; they have a sun of their own, and they know
> Stars in their own constellations. (ll. 637–41)

p. 153 'The Pieces'

This poem makes use of material concerning the early temples of Apollo at Delphi. In the writings of Pausanias (c. AD 150), there is the following account:

> They say that the most ancient temple of Apollo was made of laurel ... The Delphians claim that the second temple was made by bees from beeswax and feathers, and that it was sent to the Hyperboreans by Apollo ... It is not so very strange that the third temple was made out of bronze, seeing that Acrasius made a bedchamber of bronze for his daughter, that the Spartans still

> have a sanctuary of Athena of the Bronze House, and that the Roman forum possesses a bronze roof. The rest of their account I cannot credit: either that this temple was the work of Hephaestus, or the story about the 'golden singers' mentioned by Pindar in his verses ... Nor do I find the accounts agree about how this bronze temple disappeared: some say it fell into a chasm in the earth, others that it was melted by fire. (*Description of Greece* 10.5.9.–12.)

I have drawn on the lines by Pindar mentioned here; they are these:

> The walls were bronze, and bronze
> Columns stood beneath them:
> Up on the pediment, six golden
> Singers cast their spell.
> But when the sons of Cronos
> Opened the earth with thunder,
> They buried that most sacred of all works,
> Amazed at the sweet singing –
> For travellers were dying
> Far away from their children
> And their wives, having set their hearts
> On that song, mellifluous, addictive.
>
> (Pindar, *Paean* 8 (fr. 521), ll. 68–79)

p. 166 'Coda'

The lines of Greek at the head of this poem are the first two in a fragment of Pindar. Other poems in *The House of Clay* also make use of this fragment. According to Plutarch, Pindar's subject in the lines is the abode in Hades of the pious dead:

> For them, beneath us while the night is here,
> There blazes down the power of the sun;
> In fields crimson with roses
> They have their suburbs, with their shady trees
> Of frankincense [ ] and other trees
> Weighted with golden fruit.
> Some take delight in horses, some
> In exercises, some in games of draughts,

Others in the music of lyres,
And happiness is common to them all
In its full bloom, completely.
Across the lovely country the scent
Spreads out, from offerings of every kind
They mix on the gods' altars
With fire, seen burning from far off.

(*Threnos* 7 (fr. 129), ll. 1–10)

Torchlight (2011)

p. 176 'Oxford Poetry'

The second section of this poem quotes from Sir Alec Douglas-Home's 'Secret & Personal' memo as Foreign Secretary to the Prime Minister Edward Heath of 13 March 1972 (Public Records Office).

p. 188 'Hymn'

The ancient Greek *Hymn to Demeter* is one of the so-called Homeric Hymns, mythological poems (of varying lengths) which seem to have been parts of the repertoire of Homeric performers from early times. Scholars date the *Hymn to Demeter* to the sixth century BC. My translation of the *Hymn* attempts to be as faithful as possible to the Greek text. I have, however, made some cuts and compressions; I have also translated a number of epithets in ways not quite in line with what we can know about their 'literal' meaning; and occasionally I have erased particular epithets altogether. I have worked from the text of Martin L. West's *Homeric Hymns, Homeric Apocrypha, Lives of Homer* (Cambridge, MA, 2003), alongside the text and commentary of N.J. Richardson's *The Homeric Hymn to Demeter* (Oxford, 1974).

p. 203 'Sappho fr. 58'

In 2004, the wrappings of an Egyptian mummy in the collection of the University of Cologne were found to contain pieces of the Greek text of Sappho (sixth century BC). One fragment in particular related to scraps of a poem discovered among the Oxyrhynchus papyri in 1922, and known since then as fr. 58: by combining the Cologne text with the existing fr. 58, scholars have produced what may well be a substantially complete lyric by Sappho. The poem appears to be in six two-line stanzas, with a few words still missing only in the first four lines. The Greek text, with a translation by Martin L. West, was published in the *Times Literary Supplement* on 24 June 2005.

p. 211 'Riddarholmskyrkan'

The Riddarholmen Church in Stockholm, located on an island close to the Swedish Royal Palace, contains the tombs of Swedish monarchs from the early seventeenth century onwards.

Index of Titles

44A 160
1966 213

About Lisbon 56
Academic Sentences 57
Adam's Dream 63
The Aftermath 69
Against the Fear of Death 144
Air and Angels 78
An Alarm 101
An Eclipse 52
The Anniversary 147
Arithmetic 158
As Seen 124
At Castlereagh Church 76
At Rosses Point 94
Augury 184
August 93
The Authorities 66

The Back Roads 116
The Battery Boy 213
The Bees 163
Bits and Pieces 216
Bitter 45
The Blood-Bruise 101
Blue Skies 215
The Brancusi Room 46
Breakfast 45
Broken 211

Canopic Jars 180
Cash Positive 7
A Castaway 185
Cetacea 126
The Cheetah 220
Childhood Memories 213

China 23
Clearout 127
The Cloud 93
The Collar 216
The Company 115
The Conversion 103
Coda 166
Count Dracula Entertains 10
Country 204
The Creatures 48
The Cup 74

Damon the Mower 109
De Gustibus 66
The Deaf Wars 27
The Dedication 68
Deception 10
Delaval 54
The Difference 186
The Dog 3
Draught 179

The Earthquake 57
Eclogue 112
Eidolon 59
Endtime 44
Ether 4

A Fall 102
Fireworks 110
First Light 13
First Principles 57
Five Circumstances 50
Flex 149
The Fob-Watch 143
Forecast 149
Foreknowledge 80
Friday 80
From the Porch 51
The Full House 106

Galatea 8
A Gift 11
The Glass Harmonica 56
The Glen 47
A Gloss 75
The Gnat 128
Grace Before Meat 22
The Green, Grassy Slopes of the Boyne 31
Green Tea 173

The Hand 122
The Hands of Juan Peron 29
The Harbour 187
A Hard Place 47
[Heart] 181
A History Channel 89
Hush 105
Hymn 188

Ideal Home 15
In Heaven 146
In His Place 69
In the Hall of Mirrors 17
In the Sketchbook 68
The Interruption 178
Intestines 181
Inventory 148
Isis 138

Jordan 139

Kenneth 217
Killers 17

Lagan 139
Late Morning 152
Later 183
Least 212
Least Harm 89
Lights 180

Lines on the Demolition of the *Adelphi*, 1937 70
Literal 129
Liver 180
The Long Look 95

Mahogany 25
Mar Sarkis 145
Meissen 41
The Mild Autumn 104
The Moth 131

The Neighbours 169

Ode 160
On a Good Day 42
On Show 55
The Other World 132
Out of Ireland 14
The Overcoat 134
Oxford Poetry 176

A Pair of Shoes 175
Paprika 4
The Passions 53
Pastoral 76
The Pattern 140
A Pause 67
Peacetime 49
Penalty 188
Petrol 215
The Pieces 153
Point A 58
Point B 63
Portrush 183
A Prism 26
The Proof 116

Quis Separabit 151

Rainbow Ribbons 1980 172

The Reeds 172
Reno 43
The Resurrection of the Soldiers 90
Reversing Around a Corner 171
Riddarholmskyrkan 211
The Risk 103
The Rival 67
The Road to Rome 95

San Domenico 121
Sappho fr. 58 203
Saturday ['Wellington, Blenheim, Spitfire, Hurricane'] 82
Saturday ['We would leave the band practising noisily'] 218
Seashells 106
The Scald 77
A Schoolboy 136
Short Story 5
The Signal 15
Silent Night 18
Singles 170
The Situation 41
Slowest 182
Some Figures 6
The South 16
Souvenir d'Ypres 214
Spartans 217
Spillage 92
Spoils 133
The Stand-Off 108
Standstill 102
Still 7
Still Life 25
The Street Called Straight 158
Strongman 132
Sunday 86
Sunday in Great Tew 34
Survivors 22
Swimmer 12
Syrian 142

Tercets 26
The Third Day 33
This Earth 219
The Thread 108
Three Rivers 138
Tommy 218
Torchlight 214
Totalled 28
Travellers 94
The Twilight Summit 9
Two Memorials at Gilnahirk 91
Two Spiders 105
Two Trees 73

The Victory Weekend 80
Vigilantes 159
Visitors 75
A Volume of Memoirs is Forthcoming 24

The Wait 203
The Walk 150
Walking in the Garden 61
War Diary 130
The Watercolourists 117
The Way to Lose 109
The Weather 169
Windows 137
Words for a Poem 92
Work: 1958 79
Work: 1998 107
Wrong 8

Index of First Lines

A bitter taste, and the tongue constrained always in the mouth 66
A door too low to be a door 140
A drive along Belfast's eastern strip 151
A flat right hand: four fingers and a thumb 122
A row of figures on the mantel, not yet of any particular value 57
A sound from above like ripped material 184
A spoon palms, cups her face 22
A typist has got it wrong, and so in pen 177
A whole year since 147
Across the Lisburn Road, every other wall was marked 217
After so many drawings 63
Against the Baltic Sea 211
All around the lip, twisting and winding, tendrils of ivy 74
Alone, where there is no etiquette to breach 54
Already, on the hills 13
Although the ground 61
And now they tell me that the old girl's dying 24
As he stares at the peeled head 46
As I look now, you are starting to look through me 106
As I walked to the appointment with you at my heels 110
As our black Ford Prefect rumbled from Stranmillis 213
As soon as you open the front door 15
As the car boils 144
At dawn, the gulls call out to one another 101
At day's end, in a lull beneath stained and watery heavens 48
At last there was time to dream again 5
At noon, in the building that has no daylight 43
At six, we went to drink beer on the roof 80
At the mid-point of a working day 172

Behind them, the radio surges 4
Being obliged to climb higher, there is nothing else for it 53
Beside a road that belts through the desert 142
Boundless east wind 150
Bowed down, bowed under 132
But for the time, I would tell you 183

Cat-shaped, but bigger than a cat 220
Children, take your fill of the good things 203
Clutching his sides at the very mention of the name 7

Don't wake them; they have been asleep too long 26
Down, step by step, and along the bumpy path 139
Dust in the umbrella pines 95

Each night when they bring her face to face 8
Enough just to be there 89
Even if she had asked him, the blue girl, what 8
Everything he touched, it fell to pieces 41

For decades, when you think of Union Street 106

Half-daylight, and the summer stars 131
Half-way down you lose the sense of falling 49
Half-way up, on the inside, here 77
Hardly another car on the whole road 79
He runs cold water into a glass 179
He was stuck fast, I suppose, in his twenties 91
He would see you coming half-way up Dunluce Avenue 218
Hidden again from view 180
How everything cools and calms, how it all 149
How long is it now since the two of us 26
How slightly, twenty years ago 108

I am making believe I 204
I am not speaking 59
I cut and press the five blood oranges 45
I didn't see it, although I heard about it later 215
I don't know if they ever met in life 183
I sampled the priest's home-brew 145
I wake up from a dream about being in America 102
I walked home in the dark and beneath trees 52
I was trying to read, but the terrible lights and splatter 93
I was trying to recall, and find words for 160
I worked against it all that afternoon 101
I'm back, and the mild autumn is here too 104
If I searched, my search for it was brief 143

If I watch any more, I'll start to be seen 89
If they had names once, their names are not to be spoken 45
If you sat here long enough 51
Imagine the scene 9
In the single-bedroom flat I used to cry the night through 169
It is not genius at all: rather, a certain facility 67
It is not the man within 149
It is six in the evening in the nineteenth century 117
It is true: knowledge is indeed matter for advancement 66
It must be warm weather, for the front door and the hall 215
It seemed too long to wait, and the queue, a dozen deep 15
It was a good half-century after the battle 214
It was going to take four of us at least 29
It was the first morning after the earthquake 63
It's as though the fields around these parts 112
It's nearly over now 27
It's summer now, or nearly. Out at the back door, my sister 18
It's time to get back to the car. Already, at half-past three 34

Just as he'd told them every Christmas 23
Just how far do you have to go 14

Last night I dreamed he came back from the dead 94
Later, he thought about all the disguises 187

Maps on tables are charts of losses, ruin 69
My grandmother's grave is heaped with roses and carnations 217
My head is melting 33
My road from the bus-stop 121

Near the beginning, it must be a summer's day 93
Next morning, we slip back out 22
Night after night, my stare fixed itself on the dark 92
No sign of me 152
Not everybody is happy, or loved 47
Now it starts 56
Now the city is almost completely empty 56

Of course the walls are silent, but 90
On a scooped-out wall, far underground 95

On his annual visits from Stranraer, my uncle Tom 216
On my own now with the lake, lake-water's 172
Once I had lost you, you became 211
One birthday I came to see you out of the blue 116
One by one, without show, and almost meticulously 69
One February night, my father came home shaking 216
Or, alternatively 31
Our taxi sails on an open road 133
Outside, a light shuffle 212

Page upon page of the abandoned and the lost 68
Pencil strokes shine like pewter or gunmetal 175
Plato could have handled it: the turns 171
Power-cuts in the strike added a new dimension 214

Reader, I am the ghost of Robert Adam 70
Resourceful as he was, he seemed destined 186
Rewound here, and closed in 181
Running like that, his arm in hers 75

She lives now in an unbuilt 58
So much to be got rid of, that will go 127
So up he got, moving numb legs and arms 128
Somebody almost takes the call 178
Speak these words, in this order, pause 105
Spring this week came breezing in 76
Stung, twisting in 12

Tail-feathers on the kitchen floor 153
That morning, when I was half-way 173
That nothing comes or goes at this hour 80
The beer in my fist is a bar of gold, and bitter 109
The ceiling makes itself a low arch 158
The chances are this won't work 103
The clouds are blue with electricity and rain 188
The clouds were following one another south 6
The costumes are a kind of late-colonial 28
The distance starts to glow 146
The dog lay there with one leg missing 3
The first has been dead for a long time 105

The first time I ever saw a man riding a horse 213
The flat road with no corners and no end 44
The house of stone 124
The light of the new moon and every star 130
The light of the sun 166
The little girl who meets me in the tomb 75
The maker of necklaces turns his back 11
The map in my hands is done 94
The narrow and wide streets were trodden grass 86
The narrow channel they call Neptune's Bellows 10
The piece of paper (one piece of paper) 92
The road might as well be made from sun and water 78
The shadow over your shoulder 42
The square shop window (not really 137
The story may not be true, of course: that pair 16
The struggle of the fly 136
The sun goes out in pink and purple 76
Then in September came the plague of spiders 103
There and then, he takes a big breath 126
There is a house where all the doors are closed 102
There is a sad place, where everything is resolved 50
There is, first, the disappointment of a case 55
There was a garden behind the labourers' cottage 47
These buildings are heartbroken for the city 107
They drink cold wines by the side of a river 25
They stand guard at the invisible gates 159
They would bury ashes or bodies in the evening 203
They're not all old, and he's about my age 115
This cannot be seen, and accordingly 57
This is about Demeter, the long-haired goddess 188
This jar contains my heart 181
Those lovers in the attic 4
To say anything now is to risk it all 108
To speak exactly about the situation is difficult 41
To think that it should come to this 17
To work it through, the brain is just 158
Today there's a blind slop of oils 25
Tonight again I thought I could see your face crying 109
Two telephones all morning giving each other hell 7

Unfortunately, it was never simple 10
Unprotected for the most part, out of their paper sleeves 170

We are close now, it may be, to the delicate matter 67
We saw the big grey fish deep in the river 139
We stop, and doors come open then 134
We would leave the band practising noisily at school 218
Weeds upon weeds, sticky with cables and jags 73
Weightless to me, the heavy leaves 169
Wellington, Blenheim, Spitfire, Hurricane 82
When he was washed up naked on the shore 185
When Piranesi scrubbed the plate clean of its dedication 68
When the first rockets tore 182
When the last of the sunlight goes 163
When they had done their job 180
When you were born, the night sky broke to let fall 138
Whenever I talk to them, they don't answer: maybe 219
White walls and ceilings; a pallor of wood 148
Who looks out with an equal mind 160
Why should it be the flesh 129
Wild grasses, bleached, miles of them 132

You could think of them as hunters 17
You had come so close, that when I woke 116
You weren't there, but your typescript had arrived 176